Business
Basics

Starting and operating a business in Australia

Joe Hunt

BB Publications

Published by:

BB Publications

admin@bbpublications.com.au

Author:

Joseph Kenneth Hunt CPA

Cover design:

Tom Norrish

Printed by:

Quality Press, Welshpool. Western Australia

Copyright

© 2021 BB Publications

ISBN: 978-0-646-84811-2

CONTENTS

1. INTRODUCTION

BOOK STRUCTURE
AUTHOR

This is a down-to-earth look at going into and running businesses.

It's set in an Australian context, allowing targeted comments on taxes, laws, and regulations.

There is no championing silver bullets, tricks, or magic panaceas for instant and fabulous success; that means presuming personal capacities and motivations. It also implies magic exists.

It offers information, explanations, and ways of analysing and thinking about things. It helps identify opportunities and challenges.

Topics are broken into such basic elements that what to do and how to do it becomes obvious.

For those going into business for the first time, any fog on what to think about will clear.

For those already underway, most of what's ahead will already be known – it's 'basic'. Start-up sections aren't relevant. But there will be new bits of knowledge, another angle to old problems, or a nudge to be more practical.

If only seeking to understand why businesses do what they do, read on. There are wonderfully smug feelings ahead when the rest of the party is incredulous at an apparent business absurdity.

BOOK STRUCTURE

Chapters trace a journey through the stages:

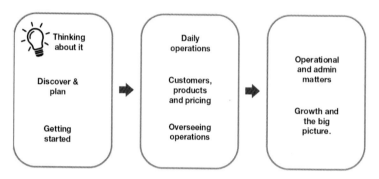

Each chapter covers a single topic and is structured to stand alone, so skipping one here and there has little impact on understanding the others.

For navigating through the book's topics, use the Contents listing flicked past to get to this page.

To see the subjects covered in each topic, use the list of sections at the beginning of each chapter.

All chapters and sections are listed together at the end of the book providing a more detailed index and a broader overview.

AUTHOR

Entry to business was via an accounting degree, used extensively initially, and returned to several times since.

Public accounting has been the primary focus, with spells as a partner and sole practitioner. There have been a few forays into larger corporate work.

There are not many types of businesses not helped with purchasing, starting up, running, expanding, closing, or selling. Also, not many ownership types or motivations for being in business, not met up with.

A stint as CEO gave responsibility for outcomes needing to be achieved by others - an intense hands-on application of strategising, monitoring, and motivating.

There were a few years of peace operating a country store. There was a 12-bedroom guesthouse on a sensational piece of coastline for seven years and a seven-day-a-week café for four years.

The last eleven years of full-on work were spent back on the accounting path, designing, and implementing, major software systems for government agencies.

These experiences have happened in eight cities and towns in three states, plus overseas spells in the Isle of Man and Bashkortostan.

The result is a clear understanding that nothing in business is mysterious or magical – only logical and transparent. Any interest in sensationalising reality has gone.

Clearly, I stopped being young a long time ago.

Business basics are broken into smaller elements until the choices are clear, the path forward requiring little more than common sense.

2. OWNING A BUSINESS

BUSINESS OR PERSONAL INTEREST
CONCEPTS OF SUCCESS
FUTURE OPTIONS
PART-TIME
WHAT INCOME IS NEEDED

Going into business is life changing. It guarantees more engagement, more control over future directions, and more satisfaction from successes.

There is satisfaction from getting more direct rewards for that extra effort, coming up with a cunning solution, or working late to meet a deadline.

Any vision of freedom over time and commitment, though, is an illusion.

So, why now? Why this opportunity?

Poor career prospects, limited employment opportunities, or a lifestyle change may be driving the move. It could be the realisation of a long-held ambition.

Whatever the primary force is, the number one underlying motivation is to make money.

Making money may be the only reason. After all, if a business can pay wages and make a profit, why not go into one and have both the wage and the profit!

But, as much as it may be about money, deciding to go into business is never purely rational, emotions need equal recognition and consideration.

BUSINESS OR PERSONAL INTEREST

Is it primarily to make a living or is it pursuing a personal interest? If it's a bit of both, which bits are they, and when they clash, which ones take priority?

Unless the reasons are clear, reactions to choices will be conflicted.

Conflicted thoughts lead to poor decisions and failure to make the available profits or satisfy personal interests and passions - and drive operators insane with self-doubt in the process.

How absurd is it that most vegetarian cafes serve only vegetarian food? If the café is a business, not a personal crusade, why wouldn't there be at least one or two choices for non-vegetarians?

How often might four people look in, then all walk on because one won't have a meal without meat? Regular restaurants cater for vegetarians!

It doesn't have to be either an entirely business or entirely personal interest. The crucial point is to clearly distinguish which one the issue under consideration is.

A skilled painter might find their landscape paintings sell well enough to provide a good income, though they don't give enough artistic challenge.

The business decision then is to paint enough landscapes each year to produce the income wanted. The personal decision is to paint what they genuinely enjoy painting for the rest of the time.

CONCEPTS OF SUCCESS

At the most fundamental level, concepts of success are either:

- Primary objectives: essential - a deal-breaker if missing.
- Secondary objectives: desirable - but life continues if they're missing.

Categorising success elements this way makes plain their importance and priority.

Making money is a primary objective. But success involves more than simply making money.

Being considerate and respectful in all dealings usually rank as primary objectives.

Maintaining community standards, helping the less fortunate, and pursuing personal interests, waiver a bit between primary and secondary.

Elements transition from primary at one end of the availability scale to secondary at the other end.

Having family time, holidays and flexible working hours is always a primary objective. But, after reaching minimum acceptable levels, additional time and flexibility become secondary.

The elements of success also sway between primary and secondary according to the abundance or scarcity of others.

For instance, is a moderate, rather than high, profit acceptable if it means more family time.

The anticipated lifespan of the business affects the balance between competing objectives.

The considerable profit of a seven-day-a-week roadhouse and motel in a remote location makes more sacrifices acceptable for a four-year plan than for a twenty-year career plan.

Getting the definition of success clear and making sure it matches the realities, is essential. Much better deciding against an opportunity than being locked into simmering disappointment.

FUTURE OPTIONS

Businesses without the flexibility to grow, contract, or exit easily add a rigid element to life – and life is neither rigid nor predictable.

Will something making so much sense now, provide opportunity for a satisfying life for the term of commitment to it?

Will it stop being satisfying and force an unwanted change somewhere in the future?

Flexibility is a hugely valuable attribute; owners can operate as they wish now and take other paths when they choose.

The following points help assess how much exists and how much is needed:

- Is it a career business? If not, how long might it operate? What skill set will exist at the finish, and how useful will that be for the next stage of life?
- Exit options: How easy will getting out be? What financial and personal impacts will it have?
- Growth: Does it offer options to grow, remain as is, or contract in harmony with changes in personal priorities.
- Diversification: Are there opportunities to develop in different directions and different markets if that becomes a wish?

A manufacturer of a tight range of products for a niche market has options to continue as is, sell as a going concern, or inject more money and energy and make bigger profits.

A franchise, for example, typically doesn't provide this flexibility because it has restrictions on products carried, trading areas, promotions, and trading hours.

PART-TIME

Part-time businesses leave operators with the capacity to take on other income sources and occupations.

They exist to either make extra money now or as a step towards going full-time.

A hobby or personal interest that produces money now and again is not a part-time business.

If primarily for extra money now, has a part-time job been dismissed too readily? Maybe the cost of setting up a business, or the long-term commitment to it, makes the tedium of packing supermarket shelves more acceptable?

A trap for part-time businesses wanting the option to transition to full-time is to establish them on non-sustainable foundations such as below-market prices or over-servicing customers.

When prices and servicing change to full-time levels, customers attracted by the part-time (bargain) levels gradually disappear, and a new client base needs establishing from scratch.

Inefficient or costly production times and methods are acceptable in a part-time operation when there is no intention of going full-time. They are also okay if it's only an interim position, and investment in more efficient production methods forms part of a transition to full-time.

Part-time operators planning to become full-time need to establish on pricing and service levels consistent with full-time realities.

WHAT INCOME IS NEEDED

Going into business changes personal and family finances.

Business plans only estimate profit from the business; it takes further measures to assess the personal financial effect.

A few points to consider in predicting the effects on personal finances are:

- How much is currently coming in: current annual salary and the employer superannuation contributions. What are the direct work-related costs such as daily fares, specific clothing, memberships, etc.?
- Changed living conditions: does it involve moving home? What effect on accommodation and family expenses?
- Rent for an existing property: If the plan is to operate on property already owned, does it mean going without rent or other income.
- Family vehicles: Is there an impact on the number, type, and use of private vehicles?
- Return on capital: Is the money being contributed to the business going to cause a loss of future investment income?
- Start-up period: there is a once-only start-up cost from loss of earnings between ceasing employment and the first day of operations.

The above points produce a cold hard figure of changes in the overall financial position. Emotional perspectives are separate considerations.

The financial position needed to motivate a commitment is different for everybody. Does it seem enough for the risks, changes, pressures, and rewards?

Owning and operating a business is not for everyone, and even for those it is, not every time in their life is a suitable time.

Deciding to go into business means balancing present and future interests and responsibilities with financial and personal capabilities.

3. COMMITTING

BUSINESS PLAN
DUE DILIGENCE
EXISTING BUSINESSES
RED TAPE

Committing: the final, irreversible action before jumping in, requires positive answers to a few basics:
- Will it provide the income, security, and lifestyle wanted?
- Is it within financial, physical, and management abilities?
- Is it the best thing to do with that amount of money, effort, and personal angst?
- Is this choice going to block an even better opportunity in the future?

Risk-assess every move.[1] What're the chances of an approach being wrong? What are the consequences if it is?

Researching facts and thoughts and putting the idea out to be seen and studied has more chance of exposing weaknesses

BUSINESS PLAN

A business plan is all thoughts in one clear picture.

---

[1] Caution isn't always an operator's friend, but recklessness never is!

It shows the products or services being offered, their sources, target markets, operating base, who will do the work, how long it will take to develop the market, etc.

It has a compelling narrative on why the market is going to take up this new player.

A finished plan ends up resembling a conversation with a close confidante, convincing them they needn't be concerned; the proposal is carefully, intelligently, and coolly thought through.

It is a picture of the real story, not what a prospective interested party might want to see.

To review a business plan, apply the following three steps, in the order listed:

- Common-sense. Does the story make sense? Does it fit with general concepts of availabilities, processes, and market acceptance?
- Integration. Are the profit projections and cash flow forecasts integrated with the story? Drill into a few points to see an absolute link between the proposed and the financial outcomes presented.
- Validation. Now, carry out the due diligence.

Preparing a plan is a practical exercise, not another formality to overcome on a path to a decision already made.

DUE DILIGENCE

Despite looking and feeling sensible, any proposition is too risky to rely on until the reliability of its facts and figures are established.

Due diligence is a thorough review and verification of facts, figures, and logic to establish that reliability.

It is necessary on the plan, on agreements with the vendors of the business, with intended suppliers and with significant customers.

Due diligence needs applying to any figure or piece of information where detailed personal knowledge doesn't exist.

Is the proposed principal supplier planning to set up a retail outlet in the same suburb; are they about to close their local branch, are they on the verge of insolvency?

Is the local council formulating re-zonings affecting future plans?

Maybe there is an alternate product about to hit the market. Why has no one else filled the market gap identified?

The first thing to do due diligence on is the width and depth of your ability to identify what needs investigation. Maybe bounce a few principals off a challenging listener (not a reinforcer) and see how the conversation goes.

Check those fundamental facts held as unassailable truths.

Accountants, business advisers, and industry-specific experts are essential yet costly. They should be used to expose matters needing investigation; then, step back and decide whether the planners have the skills to find the answer themselves.

Carrying out as much legwork as possible saves money and increases familiarity with the minutiae.

If the due diligence reveals the plan is not worth proceeding with, the sooner it is revealed, the better.

Find the deal-breaker items, find what they are most dependent on, and see they're okay before spending time and money on an issue that is later made redundant.

EXISTING BUSINESSES

There are advantages in buying an existing business: established markets, equipment, inventory, and promotion in place, and it's earning money from day one.

But there are also few times when consulting an accountant or business advisor is more necessary.

Simply defining what the purchase is of reveals a minefield:

- Is it the assets and transfer of the lease to the premises?
- If it's buying an incorporated entity (that operates the business), what liabilities (including unknown ones) will come with it?
- What portion of the business's income comes from the owners' labours rather than an intrinsic value of the business?
- Buying a share of a business raises issues around management control, historic liabilities emerging, and compatibility with the other owners.
- Are arrangements with suppliers and customers secure, and will they transfer securely?
- Is all the equipment owned by the vendor, or is some of it leased, hired, or provided by suppliers?
- If the sale includes a vendor's non-competing agreement, how well does that suit the direction intended for the future?
- How will personal knowledge of the vendor be made available?

Statements made by the vendor, or facts assumed from observation, need thorough due diligence. Are the stated contracts in place and ongoing? Are all permits in place and renewable?

RED TAPE

This subject doesn't comfortably fit anywhere in this book, which is ironic because it doesn't fit comfortably in businesses either.

Red tape takes time, is not always clear if it applies, and is challenging to understand. But the sooner and better it is understood and accepted, the easier operations become.

To feel indignation, consider that when the government began taxing the final user of goods and services (GST), they legislated that business operators collect it.

They give no reward for carrying out this massive task and use a big stick if when its messed up.

For more indignation, consider that employees pay income tax as they receive their income, not quarterly or annually like others. Because it's much easier for the tax office, businesses collect it.

So, again, a costly service is provided to the government for free.

Governments, though, are not the only causes of red tape; endless licences, permits, proof of qualifications, insurances, statistics, professional memberships, approvals, etc., etc., are needed to run even the simplest business.

Better to spend energy discovering what is needed and getting on with the job. Maybe also coming up with an equitable allocation of the pain and suffering between the operators.

If there isn't the time to complete red tape when it's due, what naïve hope expects more time in the future? Surrender and get it done before the due date, not under the pressure and inflexibility of being overdue.

Businesses do tasks of no benefit to them, for no reward, but spending valuable emotions on this absurdity or injustice is just plain wasteful.

Government and industry services are available for advice and direction on what to do and help clarify thoughts.

There is also an army of accountants, advisers, and industry specialists, ready and able to assist.

4. SHARING PROFITS

CAPITAL CONTRIBUTED
USE OF ASSETS CONTRIBUTED
INTELLECTUAL PROPERTY
COMMERCIAL VALUE OF SKILLS
TIME COMMITMENT
PERSONAL SERVICES

This topic looks at sharing profits and rewards equitably (not necessarily evenly) between unrelated owners.

It has little or no relevance where the owners are a married or de facto couple or have close family ties - inequities are more likely to be settled along the lines of personal relationships and income tax considerations.

It's of no relevance to anyone owning and operating on their own.

It looks particularly at situations where all owners do not own the assets, or each owner's time and personal contribution are different.

Recognising inequities is essential amongst unrelated parties.

The personal goodwill, excitement, and uncertainty that owners commence with might push any irritation of uneven contributions to the background, but eventually, the trials and monotony of operations will bring them to the fore.

Even in daily management, the bigger contributor has more influence, through emotional guilt or blackmail, unless fairly compensated for that additional contribution.

For all the above reasons, it's usual for agreements to be put in place to reward excess contributions by individual owners before sharing the balance of profits evenly.

CAPITAL CONTRIBUTED

Profit-sharing is usually proportionate to the risk of loss, not value contributed. Typically, the risk of loss is the same for all owners, so profits get shared equally.

When the capital contributed by owners is not identical, the challenge is to compensate for excesses while keeping the risk of loss equal.

Recording the excess as loans rather than capital contributed is one solution. Typically, this results in:

- Allocating interest on the excess contributions before distributing the remaining profit evenly amongst all owners[2].
- Giving the owner/lender a right for repayment of the excess portion of their contributions ahead of equal distribution of remaining value, in the event of **insolvency.**

[2] There are legal and bookkeeping implications in any non-standard profit-sharing arrangement that almost certainly need professional consultation before entering.

USE OF ASSETS CONTRIBUTED

When one owner contributes the use of an asset, either permanently or periodically, there is a case for rewarding that owner over and above normal profit-sharing.

Reward (payment) is for the gradual reduction of its value, due to either time or use, and any operating costs not borne by the business.

It wouldn't include payment for time the owner normally contributes.

Usually, payment is a standard annual amount for permanent use, and a per-use or per-hour rate for occasional use.

One example is paying a fixed monthly amount for full-time use of a forklift. Another is hiring a crane from an owner on a wet rate (supply and operate) for a once-only task.

Payment for premises, used but not owned by all owners, is discussed in a later chapter specifically on premises.

INTELLECTUAL PROPERTY

The contribution of personally created intellectual property (IP) raises immediate and long-term equity issues.

There is no issue when the IP has no saleable value, won't have any in the future, and is one of the owners' many contributions. A spreadsheet for employee rostering fits this category.

It is more complex when the business is going to:
- Further develop, then exploit the IP.
- Market it at the present level of development.
- Market it with ongoing upgrading, adaptation, and provide user support.
- Base operations on what the IP can do.
- Use the IP as a central and critical point of difference.

Issues to resolve, from the business's position, are:

- Is complete ownership being contributed?
- Is a licence to use being transferred?
- If licencing, does the owner have the right also to grant licences to others?
- What security is there over continued use?
- Is the creator the only person able to maintain and upgrade it?
- What safety, and arrangements, are there over continued support?
- Who is liable for upgrades and maintenance?
- What happens to it if the business changes hands?
- Is there a right to sub-license or make access available to customers and suppliers?
- If the value improves, who gets the benefit?

COMMERCIAL VALUE OF SKILLS

Owners' earnings in their former jobs have no influence on the balance of entitlement to profit, but not always.

If skills giving them a larger than average income are also vital to the business, additional compensation for the income loss is justifiable.

For instance, an industrial chemist joining others to produce alternative medicines, only producible under the direct supervision of a qualified person, deserves a direct reward for that contribution.

Or a geologist in a mineral exploration partnership between the geologist and a layperson could also expect an extra reward.

TIME COMMITMENT

If one owner is works sixty hours a week and another only five, or one works all year and the other only occasionally, the one doing more work deserves more reward.

Payment for extra work, ahead of the regular profit share for the extra hours, brings everyone back to level.

Alternatively, paying all owners for all the hours they work also removes the inequity.

Payment for hours worked needn't be in the form of regular employee-type wages. Legal structures typically used in small businesses make this either impossible or complicated.

One solution is to allocate profits amongst the owners, firstly to the value of work each has done, then by sharing the remainder equally.

Whether compensation, in any form, remains an entitlement when there aren't enough profits to cover it is for the owners to consider and agree upon.

PERSONAL SERVICES

In many professional and personal service practices, owners receive a percentage of their billings as their first share of profits.

The owners who also own the premises get paid rent.

And, profits remaining get shared in an agreed proportion, which, often, is not equal.

Before starting a business, roles and contributions by each owner require thorough scrutiny.

Actual and potential inequities between the owners must be equitably allowed for in the interests of fairness and long-term harmony.

5. TRADING NAME

MARKET ACCEPTANCE
ACTUAL NAMES
IDENTIFYING SERVICE & LOCATION
IDENTIFYING A PERSON
WEB PRESENCE

Operators either trade under their own names or register business names, and trade under those.

These options apply equally to individuals, groups of individuals, companies, and any other form of incorporated associations[3] and unincorporated bodies.

Incorporated entities can construct their legal name to be useful as the trading name.

Individuals can legally change their names to achieve the same. For example, a performer might change to a more marketable stage name.

---

[3] An incorporated association is an entity recognised at law as existing separately to the owners of the entity. It can sue and be sued. It can own property and trade. It could be the local young athlete's association, a chamber of commerce, a church, or a council of small business operators.

Merely registering a business name does not, in any way, create a separate legal entity.

The registry of business names reveals the owner or owners of those names. The listed owners of the name are legally responsible for all trading under that name.

Issues to resolve before deciding on a name are:

- Who the owner, or owners, are?
- Is changing their name a practical option?
- Are multiple trading names an advantage?

This chapter looks only at operational issues.

MARKET ACCEPTANCE

A trading name aids interactions with the market, so it's the effect a name has on the market, not the owners, that matters.

A business is directly associated with its name. While this is great when the name evokes desired links, it is anything but great when moving into new markets the name is too rigid to attract.

For instance, the name 'Thredbo Ski & Snowboard' creates a rigid link to the town and snow-related activities.

If the shop wanted to target hikers and campers over summer, re-positioning the name becomes a costly effort. Same again if they wanted to open a shop in another town.

Names that rely on topical wit or humour create future problems. What seems appropriate to the target market at commencement look humourless and outdated several years later. So much so, it risks alienating the same market segment of the future.

Clever puns and wordplays appeal to niche markets identified at creation but as operations evolve into broader markets, wholesaling, or exporting, what was once 'clever' now evokes an air of amateurism and insincerity.

Keep it simple, distinct enough to remember easily, easy to spell, and easy to find online.

ACTUAL NAMES

When the identity of the individual owner is important, their actual name is the easiest option. This is common in professions, personal care occupations, and the entertainment industry - for instance, Dr Phyliss Jane Harrow.

There are situations where the owner's name is of no consequence but is still a suitable and easy option. Possibilities include IT consultants, tradies, and other specialist contractors; people dealing with only a few customers and attracting work by industry contacts and word of mouth.

Companies, and incorporated entities, are required to disclose their full name on documents unless using a registered business name.

Full legal names are often inconvenient, and registering a business name is common, even if it is nothing more than an abbreviation of the legal name.

For instance, Birdsville Emporium Pty Ltd registering the name 'Birdsville Emporium'.

Using actual names for each member of a partnership is also inconvenient, especially for those needing to promote their name or with many transactions.

IDENTIFYING SERVICE & LOCATION

A business's primary signage or advertising needs to show its name, what it does, and where it is. When this information is in the name it leaves more room for other messages.

Using 'Smith & Associates Architects' Removes any need for stating the broad occupation in the ad.

Identifying location in the name offers the same brevity as industry description but capitalises on geographical advantages. For instance, Birdsville Caravan Repairs and Harley Street Lunch Bar instantly inform potential customers of place and occupation.

IDENTIFYING A PERSON

In building trades, repairers, personal care, professions, and niche retailers, it is common to use a variation of the personal name of an owner to benefit the business.

That benefit is either immediate when the name already has market recognition, or in the future when the plan is to build a brand personality behind it.

For instance, 'Smith Bookkeeping' is an appropriate name for a service connected with 'Smiths Accounting'.

The name 'Bob Smith Plumbing' let's builders know whose ute is parked on their building site more clearly than the partners' full names.

A sports store named after a sports-star owner makes sense.

Identifying a person in the trading name means the name, and therefore the personal connection, continues after the store changes hands.

When outgoing owners don't want future trade to be in their name, non-transferability of the name becomes a condition of sale. Note, though; this often negatively impacts the business's continuing recognition, devaluing its selling price.

WEB PRESENCE

Online names are created and promoted on demand and in response to individually targeted markets and current search patterns. They adapt far faster to trade opportunities than names for bricks and mortar outlets.

Flexibility and immediacy also bring risks of market disruption by other parties using misleading websites, domain names, and email addresses to capture the benefits of promotions and reputation.

Pre-emptive registering of domain names and email addresses to avoid recognisable risks of deliberate misuse is essential.

Also essential is anticipating and registering names users might presume or accidentally use, such as registering both '.com' and '.com.au' web addresses.

If the misspelling of a name or word used in an online address is common, consider registering addresses for all spellings.

If the business was previously known by a different name, it is worthwhile to add it to the addresses feeding in.

Establishing names on any digital platform, and having the feeds flow in the best possible direction, involves technical setup and regulatory issues with substantial ongoing maintenance time and money.

There is clear value in seeking professional advice on the use of social media and search engine optimisation.

A thoughtfully crafted name establishes stronger links with customers and provides more precise promotion.

Trading names need consideration of all implications for present and foreseeable activities and markets.

6. DAILY FUNDAMENTALS

BEING PROFITABLE
RELATIONSHIPS
QUALITY CONTROL
RISK MANAGEMENT
RECREATION

There are fundamental management principles behind all daily operations, and each deserves to be understood and applied continuously.

This chapter looks at a few fundamentals – some sound a bit grand for a labour-only subcontractor but still worthy of periodic consideration.

BEING PROFITABLE

The aim is to make a profit. It is not the largest turnover or the lowest cost; it is the largest difference between those two sums.

Each function requires analysing in terms of whether it is making that difference bigger or smaller.

Steadfastly increasing sales to increase profits while overlooking the cost of getting individual sales, or better use of the resources applied to get those extra sales, is not a good aim.

It is also vital to manage passion for reducing costs; it too easily mutates into a toxic affliction. Expenses earning money are to be encouraged, not limited.

RELATIONSHIPS

Each action, or thing with a public consequence, is a tool for managing relationships. And well-managed relationships make everything run better.

Relationship building permeates every decision because even minor infractions, or image contradictions, cause negative feelings in people.

For instance, flaunting local council sandwich board rules won't encourage the ranger to manage street parking to the businesses advantage; being slow to pay the plumber discourages priority attention when needed.

Personal presentations aid relationships: businesses offering serious advice have serious-looking people deliver that advice. Fashion houses have stylishly dressed staff.

Community and sporting groups seen as supported are those appreciated by, or at least not offensive to, potential customers.

And, as for feeling the need to educate a customer on how ridiculous their question is, remember that person is far more valuable than the ten other people that haven't made contact.

QUALITY CONTROL

Quality control is about maintaining a consistent quality suiting both the business and the customers.

The 'everything must be the best possible' brigade tries to link it with constant improvement; that is not what quality control is about.

Outward-facing images and actions need to convey the quality standards or do nothing to mislead the market. This gives predictability, and customers use predictability when there is a choice with whom they deal.

Delivering below a quality the customer expects leads to disappointment and therefore lost sales.

Delivering above those targets adds unplanned costs from using more expensive items or from spending too much time.

If varying from the targeted quality doesn't cause problems, those targets need reviewing. Are they relevant; are they fully aligned with the image, promotions, and operating structure?

Monitoring quality standards for consistency is essential; owners' impressions and interpretation of customer reactions are unreliable.

Non-standard actions get dismissed as exceptions unless challenged by a record showing how often those exceptions are occurring.

Customer feedback is not as much use as it might seem for quality control. It gives a sense of the level of service or product quality acceptable to existing customers; true success may mean targeting customers with different expectations.

RISK MANAGEMENT

Risk management means identifying any risk and assessing whether it is an unfixable showstopper; or to eliminate, manage, or simply ignore and live with the consequences.

For each management action, however trivial, a distinct question needs answering: can this lead to something unwanted?

It's not pessimistic or even sceptical; it's realistic. These are the elements in that question:

- What might happen?

- What are the chances of it happening?
- What are the consequences (financial, physical, reputational, time, trade interruption, etc.)?
- What will it take to rectify?
- What will it take to avoid it happening?

The matrix below shows a simple approach to risk assessment; more detailed and situation-specific matrices are available on the internet and in print.

RISK MANAGEMENT MATRIX

		Probable consequences	
	Minor - easy and cheap to fix	**Medium** - disruptive and costly to fix	**Severe** - stops operations and is financially crippling
High	Weigh up the cost of eliminating against the unpredictability and lost time.	Eliminate or have an acceptable work-around in place.	Unacceptable. Do not proceed until it is eliminated.
Medium	Monitor and carry-on.	Weigh up the cost of eliminating against the unpredictability and lost time.	Eliminate or have an acceptable work-around in place.
Low	Ignore.	Monitor and carry-on.	Weigh up the cost of eliminating against the ability to withstand an occasional hit.

(Vertical axis label: Chance of it happening)

Risk assessment is a way of life; constantly considered at any level of probability or consequence.

RECREATION

Owning a business is not about abandoning life, but without consciously structuring recreational time, everyday demands precisely cause that.

A satisfying life is almost always an essential element of success. Personal recreational time, therefore, requires a balanced whole-of-business, whole-of-life, view.

Working with little or no recreation is endurable if there is the prospect of a long break when it's over.

But, more commonly, businesses commence with an indefinite end-date, with the possibility of working it through to retirement. These need operating at a pace providing all the elements of success along the way.

Working hours, days off, holidays, and time to attend to personal matters cannot be left to chance - structures supporting the chosen work versus recreational balance need locking in place.

For instance, getting in an additional worker one day a week solely to cover the owner's absence: or booking a holiday six months in advance.

Recreation patterns need to be predictable to customers and suppliers.

The above over-arching management fundamentals are examples of the many opportunities, choices, and influences on everyday actions that, when accumulated, have an enormous effect on results.

7. EMPLOYEES

HIRING POINT
JOB DESCRIPTION
INDOCTRINATION
REWARD
SALARY PACKAGING
REVIEW ON THE FLY

Employees are either essential or desirable.

Essential because the owners lack a particular skill or quality needed.

Desirable because their existence means more money or a better lifestyle for the owners.

The primary objective for essential employees is to maximise their productivity. Highly skilled and expensive people doing unskilled tasks is a last choice.

The primary objective for desirable employees is to employ as many as possible; the challenge is finding the point at which an extra worker, or extra hours, stop adding more success.

HIRING POINT

Not enough people on the job means output suffers, standards decline, customer service suffers, and missed sales. But, on the other side, employing ahead of need means extra costs from employees being unproductive.

A level of flexibility is structured into normal staffing levels to allow for temporary absences and unexpected urgent demands on time; this flexibility absorbs the initial under-supply of people as trade increases.

When a business waits for enough work to keep another employee fully occupied, the flexibility buffer has completely disappeared, and results are suffering.

The reality is that individual employees don't need to earn more than they cost; it is enough that, overall, it is more successful by their presence.

More success includes getting additional output from freeing up revenue-generating workers and allowing owners to work on more valuable pursuits.

In other words, the point at which to put another person on is when there is more success because of their presence; fully occupying them is not a requirement.

JOB DESCRIPTION

A written description of each employee position, like multinationals and the public sector use, ensures all tasks are covered, and each position matches skills with responsibilities.

Whether or not this job description gets shared with the employee is an entirely separate point.

Decency towards others is reason enough to provide a transparent and precise description to all employees; it also obliges them to acknowledge their obligations.

Reasons for not providing a job description include:

- It does not exist, and there is no certainty for the employee.

- Some tasks are not appropriate to the role, so it's better not to document too much.
- Duties might change from day to day, and it's easier if the employee is already committed and doesn't have any solid base for negotiating.

The above reasons are not admirable.

INDOCTRINATION

Untrained and unindoctrinated employees must not get near customers alone, nor sign off on production.

Employees need to understand their duties, how they require doing, and the required standard. They need to become familiar with the culture of the business.

Training and familiarisation time needn't be entirely non-productive if close supervision or temporary work in a different or non-customer facing position is possible.

Errors or irregular standards by new employees seem acceptable to the owners when they understand why it happened. They have confidence it will be correct next time.

But that first customer, or the product user, sees what they receive – be it a new employee's first or second attempt.

REWARD

Operators choose employees to support their concepts of success. Employees choose who they work for their (own) idea of success.

Any significant mismatch will result in early terminations. Time spent profiling applicants to see if the role has what is important to them is time well spent.

For unskilled roles offering no serious career growth, good motivations for attracting and retaining the right people are money, working hours, and shift structure.

Money and working hours might be less important for skilled, professional, and career-focused people; ongoing skill and reputation enhancement become valuable rewards.

Generally, industrial awards and industry norms provide the minimum required package; when warranted, further reward gives more loyal employees.

SALARY PACKAGING

Salary packaging is about rewarding an employee in a more beneficial way than straight wages, at no additional cost.

Providing a vehicle for private use, subscriptions to sporting organisations, paying children's school fees, gifts, entertainment, holidays, etc., attract less tax to the employee. But they attract Fringe Benefits Tax[4] (FBT) for the business.

In compensation for the FBT, businesses pay less in direct wages, which is calculable to a point where the total cost is the same with or without salary packaging.

Because of differences between income tax and FBT, careful juggling of benefits and costs results in less personal tax for the employee, and therefore more money overall, at no extra cost.

Salary packaging is not typical in small businesses because of the time it takes to get in place and because of ongoing administration. It tends to suit larger workforces and those with long term employment patterns.

---

[4] Fringe Benefits Tax is paid by employers to the tax office for non-wage payments made for the personal benefit of employees.

REVIEW ON THE FLY

For instant assessment of employees, performance matrices provide instant high-level views of whether they add to or detract from success.

Fundamentally they crossmatch output to management effort to highlight:

- Below-average performers needing above-average management effort (undesirable).
- Above-average performers needing below-average management effort (desirable).
- Average performers needing average management effort (acceptable).

The following matrix is a simple example. More complex and industry-specific models are available in print and online.

PRODUCTIVITY VALUE MATRIX

Level of productivity

		Low	Medium	High
Management needed	**High**	Low producer and difficult to manage. *Probably not rescuable.*	Medium producer requiring constant management. *Barely acceptable. Offer ways to improve and review regularly.*	High producer requiring constant management. *Acceptable, but at reward levels equivalent to a medium employee.*
	Medium	Low producer needing medium management. *Barely acceptable. Offer ways to improve and review regularly.*	Medium producer needing medium management. *Sufficiently reliable and predictable.*	High producer needing medium management. *A great employee.*
	Low	Low producer needing little management. *Will not be covering costs of employment - look for ways to increase productivity or stop using.*	Medium producer needing little management. *A valuable employee.*	High producer with little management. *Employing this type of person is one of life's joys.*

Such arbitrary cross-matching is far too rough for decisive action on its own. Still, it adds illumination and perspective to workplace frustrations.

If ultimately it is decided the employee's current performance, in their current role, is not satisfactory, more guidance, support, training and role reviews are the obvious next step.

Businesses employ people to be successful.

If this is not happening, the business model is wrong, the approach to employing people isn't working, or the employees are unsuitable.

Employees are like other suppliers; the more well managed the relationship, the greater the reward.

8. OUT-SOURCING

SALES

PRODUCTION

DELIVERY AND DISTRIBUTION

OFFICE FUNCTIONS

EXIT STRATEGY

Every business outsources.

For instance, most outsource the preparation of their income tax returns: developing the skills in-house is more expensive, time-consuming, and adds management complexity.

Servicing and repairing vehicles is usually outsourced. Employing and managing a mechanic is only the start of the reasons for not doing it internally; there is also the requirement for floor space, capital equipment, ongoing tool and IT costs, and massive under-utilisation costs.

Even using a courier is outsourcing.

The challenge with outsourcing solutions is identifying those that increase success, free up management time and resources, improve product volume and range, broaden market scope, or reduce costs.

Advantages of new outsourcing propositions need balancing with the time, effort and inconvenience of new support processes. These are not always obvious and often ignored or underplayed by the outsourcer.

Outsourcing production typically involves using the provider's equipment to save capital outlay. It provides access to larger capacity and more sophisticated processes, enabling additional volumes and products.

Outsourcing charges include recovery for the suppliers' equipment, which is a problem if it under-utilises existing equipment.

The following topics show a variety of approaches to analysing outsourcing propositions.

SALES

Outsourcing doesn't always involve the entire range of goods or services. Individual markets get outsourced, as do selected products and services.

One life cycle stage, such as start-up, or decline, may be outsourced to compensate for the higher costs of selling small volumes.

Outsourcing helps when a physical location or a chosen marketing approach restricts expansion into distant markets.

Disguising and promoting products sold through an outsourcer as alternatives to the existing product enables more targeted strategies for different market segments. Also, a business's best competitor is itself.

Developing new products or markets risks awakening demand for more quantities than the business's capacity to sell and distribute, creating a gap for competitors to fill. Outsourcing enables faster penetration of all markets.

Outsourcing invariably comes at a cost by way of lower returns per unit sold; meaningless though if it means more success overall.

Outsourcing sales creates risks when it also separates product promotion from the direct control of the business.

Controls are needed to ensure distributors project an acceptable image.

PRODUCTION

Outsourcing removes the need to own, manage, and accommodate production equipment. It frees up time and energies to focus on product, brand, and market development.

Outsourcing production is more likely to occur when sales, not production, is driving profit.

Relevant outsourcing production considerations are:

- Sourcing individual products from separate producers.
- Using multiple producers for the same product.
- The geographic location of a producer does not always need to be near the centre of operations.
- Specialty producers enable a broader range of products and more variations.
- Updating for market trends and product improvements does not require expensive equipment upgrades.
- Handmade and artisan-type products require robust quality and non-competing agreements with producers.
- Remote production shortens delivery times and costs to distant markets.
- Overseas and interstate producers are in scope when delivery times are acceptable.
- When order quantities dictate the per-unit price, the practicality of the quantities needed to get the lower costs become an issue.
- Outsourcing helps existing production capacity to handle temporary excess production demands.

Sales of made-to-order products are limited to quantities producible between receiving the order and an acceptable delivery date. Outsourcing increases production capacity, increasing the number of products producible in this time frame.

Outsourcing means disclosing product details to capable producers and risking their misuse of it. This risk is either acceptable, manageable by agreements and controls, or completely unacceptable.

Agreements range from using pre-existing standard terms of an established supplier to being as unique and complex as engaging artisans to produce to an exacting standard.

DELIVERY AND DISTRIBUTION

Outsourcing delivery and distribution leave the business to focus on what makes it what it is, and it allows smooth and unlimited growth of distribution volumes.

A business need never see their product after producing it. They need never see it at all if importing or outsourcing manufacture.

Logistics companies pick-up and receive products, warehouse them, and maintain inventory controls linked to the business's internal systems and online portals.

At a full integration, stock is picked and forwarded to the customers when sold, based entirely on IT system interfaces.

Delivery times are shortened by leveraging the logistics company's skills and resources and having stock warehoused in their network of warehouses, enabling earlier delivery across more localities.

Logistic companies, having large delivery volumes, negotiate lower per-item delivery costs. Passing this on to customers is an added sales attraction.

For example, Amazon's per-item delivery price can be lower than a small business pays (and on-charges to customers), making it cheaper to buy from Amazon.

It is also possible to outsource delivery by leveraging an existing operator, usually one servicing the same market.

For instance, a fishing bait supplier may arrange with a crushed ice retailer (both require freezer delivery, and the markets overlap) to deliver bait to retail outlets.

On the negative side, the more comprehensively warehousing and distribution functions get outsourced, the more it costs per unit and the more inventory required.

On the positive side, outsourcing delivery and distribution increases the capacity to sell products.

OFFICE FUNCTIONS

Small operations may look at outsourcing to a bookkeeping service to do the pays, issue sales invoices, chase up slow payers, record and pay supplier accounts, reconcile bank accounts, lodge the BAS return, and update the central ledger recording.

For those not doing their bookkeeping well, outsourcing is not the answer. Only repeatable functions get successfully outsourced, not the personal discipline to retain the source information and have it readily accessible and understandable.

Answering to the demands and costs of the bookkeeping service encourages personal discipline – and much of the benefit is due to that improved discipline.

Outsourcing bookkeeping is worthwhile when the rewards from freeing up owners' time justify it.

EXIT STRATEGY

What is involved in getting out of an outsourcing arrangement? Regardless of how simple or complex it is, outsourcing arrangements need to have workable exiting options in place before beginning:

- What notice of cancellation will the outsourcer give?
- How will vital information be gotten from the outsourcing service, particularly if it's a hostile break?
- If transferring the outsourcing to another provider, how much cooperation is to be relied on?
- What if the provider goes bust?
- If the provider defaults on elements such as quality and timeliness, what are the rights to terminate?
- Maybe they change the services they offer, or raise the price too much?
- Perhaps, after the completion of a contract term, no renewal is available?
- How easy will it be to re-assume the function if needed?
- How enmeshed is that supplier in relationships with suppliers, customers, websites, and markets?

For each negative answer above, means submitting to the provider's mercy or risking a stressful disaster down the track.

Outsourcing is an obvious solution to tasks outside existing skills or capacity.

There are also strategic advantages in outsourcing tasks within the existing skills or capacity.

Every proposition needs thorough and objective consideration because similar seeming situations will range from being too expensive and overwhelming to the best thing that ever happened.

9. LIFE CYCLES

MARKET

CUSTOMERS

PRODUCT

EQUIPMENT

BUSINESS OWNERS

IMAGE

PREMISES

All aspects of business are relentlessly transitioning through life cycle stages. Principally:

- Introduction.
- Productiveness.
- Decline.

Each stage has different impacts on markets, customers, inventory and operations – what's best for one stage isn't necessarily best for the next stage.

Continuing to do the same thing the same way risks it having an increasingly declining value.

Knowing the current stage of the cycle, how rapidly and in what direction it is changing, is critical.

And, understanding each life cycle means understanding the entire product and market realities, where to focus now and whether to still focus on it a year from now.

Internal statistics and customer surveys support the interpreting of life cycle changes but aren't a substitute – they reveal the current situation, not where it is heading.

Following are life cycles that are generally applicable.

MARKET

Potential customers get grouped into categories, for example, by age, gender, occupation, income, and marital status; anything providing narrower and more targeted marketing.

And each group has a life cycle.

A mountain bike retailer might find their teenage market is in the decline stage, and their 40 to 60-year-old market is booming through the productive stage.

Marketing efforts for the teenagers will focus on renewing interest and on creating interest for the older group.

Identifying the stage and size of each market group enables predicting a product's market direction over the next one, five, or ten years.

CUSTOMERS

Apart from seasonal and short-term buying patterns, customers' demand is related to their current interests, fashion sense, location, income, and family situation – their stage in life.

Recognising the driving force behind a customer means predicting how long they may be in that market. This information is especially valuable where the customer pool is definable.

For instance, a shop targeted children's needs in an aging suburb will anticipate a declining market pool – the area they draw from is clearly defined and more and more people in that area are moving into post-children stages of life.

Customers also have life cycles within the time they stay with a business. Progression could be through; cautious introduction, enthusiastic shopper, loyal and trusting, habitual, disinterested, and finally, receptive to change.

Recognising the stages of individual customers enables targeted promotion, or attention, or loyalty initiatives. Refreshing interest at strategic stages extends the time they remain customers.

PRODUCT

Individual products and services have life cycles around how long they remain in fashion or how long they stay chosen as the best fit for the purpose they serve.

Knowing a product's life cycle stage is critical in assessing its ongoing prospects; in allocating promotional effort, shelf space, training, storage, and management attention.

For instance, a software specialist supporting an application already becoming redundant might outsource their customer maintenance work rather than employ a technician in a long term and permanent position.

An employee may be more profitable in the short term, but the product life cycle indicates the position is destined to become under-utilised and, therefore, loss-making.

Everyday management decisions benefit from conscious judgement on the life cycle stage of each product and service offered.

EQUIPMENT

Time and use reduce the value of equipment, but life cycles also influence values.

For instance, the value of industry-specific equipment moves in tune with that industry's profitability and present life cycle stage.

Value also links to the equipment's physical life cycle. Either from eventually wearing out or the need to update appearances.

When replacing equipment is a significant effort, the closer it is to that effort, the more its resale value drops - independent of reliability or maintenance issues.

Life cycles are critical when buying more equipment or replacing existing equipment - basing decisions only on present needs risks having equipment with no market to serve or under the capacity needed.

Market life cycles enable far more strategic production capacity management, including (non-intuitive) pre-emptive upgrading for futureproofing.

BUSINESS OWNERS

'Businesses' don't go through lifecycles; owners do. Business is a label for the total parcel of related elements and only looks like a single entity when viewed from a distance.

Owners will start with nervous enthusiasm and huge aspirations driving a commitment that puts non-business issues on the back burner. Eventually though daily tasks get handled with casual confidence, and other aspects of life come back into focus.

That initial cycle may take about eighteen months. Once it's out of the way, owners have enough mental bandwidth and operational knowledge to view their commitment realistically.

In social and family circles, that initial stage is expressed as "head down, butt up, for eighteen months - then think about which way to go".

The next stage is where either complacency sets in or a steady and successful pace is maintained. Directions are now getting reviewed from the advantage of practical knowledge of operations and the market.

The owners' lifecycles, such as age, marital status, and health, deeply impact directions and operations. They require factoring into planning as much as markets, equipment, finances, and any other related influences.

IMAGE

Image is about all the ways the market gains its' perception.

It is signage, corporate colours, background music, furniture and fittings, advertising style, choice of media, staff attitudes and training, honesty, and openness - anything forming a connection between the business and the market.

All aspects of image have life cycles, though not as subject to rapid change as others. And, in many ways, they are subordinate to other lifecycles.

For instance, a car dealership's showroom fitted out two years ago as comfortable and classy for a safe and reliable car is now a negative for the current flashy and fast range that's in there.

An image, appropriate when conceived, carried into future lifecycle stages risks becoming less and less ideal. The image must suit the current lifecycle stage of the market currently targeted.

PREMISES

Premises, like image, are slaves to other cycles and particularly so for marketing and production lifecycles.

Production floor space, retail space, exposure, proximity to market, and other physical attributes are clear enough to generate motivation for change.

But a less obvious cycle is the relevance of ownership of premises.

In the development stages, leasing premises may be the only affordable option. In the mature phase, ownership becomes attractive both as an investment and from guaranteeing continued occupation.

In the final stages of the owners' career, they may choose to sell and lease back their premises. Selling releases funds for investments more suitable to their retirement plans and gives a cheaper entry point for prospective business purchasers.

There is also an opposite lifecycle for ownership at start-up where the owners had enough funds to purchase the premises outright. When moving into productivity stages and requiring more equipment and working capital, selling and leasing back the premises becomes a financing option.

Each business element is constantly progressing through life cycle stages and continuing with a position based on a past stage risks declining value from it.

10. CUSTOMERS

WHO IS THE CUSTOMER
CUSTOMER MIX
MORE OR BETTER
COST TO SERVE
PRICING STRUCTURES

Customers drive businesses, so businesses choose customers that suit their route.

Therefore, at start-up, identifying potential customers comes ahead of any commitment.

And, buying an existing business without understanding existing and potential customers is not a good move.

And an existing operator not constantly reviewing customers is merely hoping for success.

So, this topic is not about whether a customer is pleasant, loyal, large, small, corporate, retail, commercial, frequent, etc.; it's about their contribution to direction and success.

WHO IS THE CUSTOMER

The customer side of any deal has elements of a:
- Consumer (ultimate user)
- Payer

- Decision-maker

From a business's side, the customer is the decision-maker.

A person buying a coffee is all the elements.

For a child's school supplies, the child is the user and the parent payer and decision-maker.

For supplying windows and doors in residential development, the owner/occupier is the consumer, the builder the payer, and the developer the decision-maker.

Sales strategies pressure consumers and payers to influence the decision maker's decision.

Daily operations target the decision maker's ability and inclination to purchase.

So, who is the customer?

- To create the demand and steer it to the business, its consumer, payer, and decision-maker – any party influencing the final decision.
- To make the transaction happen, it's the decision-maker – the party giving the final sign-off.

CUSTOMER MIX

One major customer is utopia:
- Predictable demand cycles
- Predictable product or service requirements
- No major marketing issues
- Simple billings

Or maybe it's not a utopia to be:
- Reliant on that customer's financial stability.
- Subject to their directions and purchasing policies.
- Separated from broader market trends and innovations, making future re-entry more difficult.
- Out of touch with other customers and needing to rebuild from scratch when the relationship ends.

A comfortable customer mix is a broad range by size, location, and requirements, giving insulation from the fortunes of a single or few customers.

A ball-park industry benchmark[5] for a narrow customer base is less than ten percent of customers generating more than ninety percent of turnover.

For a narrow customer base, consider a surveyor firm earning ninety-five percent of its fees from Government contracts subject to biennial open market tenders.

For a broad customer base, consider a boutique beer brewer producing several ranges of bottled and kegged beer, integrated with a café and catering complex in a popular location, doing takeaway bottled sales, having a strong online marketing approach, and wholesaling bottles and kegs to liquor outlets, cafes, and pubs over a broad geographical area.

MORE OR BETTER

'Enough' customers are needed to succeed; how many is enough depends on effort, profit, and risk.

Increasing the number of customers is an intuitive approach to increasing profits, but changing the sales mix, or selling more to the same customers, also works.

More customers are not always an option; for instance, a café at a remote tourism attraction will not get more regardless of what they do. A commercial cleaning service in a regional centre has a fixed number of potential customers.

Changing the sales mix to sell more of the most profitable is standard strategy – the next chapter, WHAT TO CARRY, addresses this.

---

[5] In a business sense, benchmarks are various standard practices or average industry outcomes.

Selling more to existing customers is achievable by reducing the price, increasing the range, increasing customer contact, more and better service, improving business and product image, and add-on selling techniques.

It is also achievable by enhancing the product or service.

The commercial cleaner will get more from existing customers by also hiring out floor mats on a rolling replacement basis or providing and maintaining live plants and floral displays.

Better service, in terms of sales technique, product knowledge and time with customers, produces more value from existing customers – but at a cost.

There is no definitive answer to 'more or better' customers - a cost-versus benefit analysis is necessary for each situation.

COST TO SERVE

Not all customers cost the same to serve.

The manner of service makes a difference. For instance:
- Personal advice versus cashier sales.
- Over-the-counter cash and card sales.
- Telephone orders.
- Online order and payment.
- An emailed order from a customer for their regular products, with a scheduled courier pick-up.
- On-site sales visits.

Physical characteristics of products mean it takes more time to sell one range of goods over another. Electrical retailers quickly process the sale of an electric kettle but take longer for a TV that also entails getting it to the customer's car.

Demographics change the cost to serve the same product. The time it takes to sell a high-tech product varies between a tech-savvy and a non-tech-savvy customer.

A commercial customer knows the product they want, but a first-time domestic customer approaches with a solution in mind and takes time matching products to it.

It takes as long to greet the customer, set up an invoice, and process the payment for multiple product lines as it does for one.

It takes no longer to raise an invoice for one product than it takes for ten of that product, meaning it is less costly selling ten of the same product in one sale than in ten sales of one each.

For first-time customers, there is introductory time and slower dealings by the customer from lack of familiarity. Meaning it costs less to serve repeat customers than one-time-only customers.

Plus, if an account needs establishing, there is a once-only set-up time. If delivery involves servicing an off-site item, there are address or equipment details to record.

Recognising selling patterns enables factoring the varying costs to serve into marketing, pricing, and future direction.

PRICING STRUCTURES

Prices regularly vary between customers – to attract customers matching strategic directions and to align effort and profitability.

Take a hospitality and kitchen goods supplier with both household and commercial customers:

- The household customers typically spend less, require more service, and are less price-sensitive, than the commercial customers. They pay ticket price.
- Restaurants and cafes buy larger quantities and require less service. They get a discount.

- The behemoths buy much larger quantities, require little service and are seriously price sensitive. They get a more significant discount.
- Chefs buy little more than households but have strategic value as gateways to their employers. They probably get the restaurant and café discount.

When and how to structure price categories:

- Which customer groups and to what extent?
- Applying to some or all items, and some or all quantities?
- Ticket price less a discount, or cost price plus a markup?

Pricing structures are so common they hardly attract attention, such as half-price admittance to venues for children, and ten percent off for pensioners.

One price does not fit all.

Thinking about customers is like thinking about fishing. What species are wanted, what bait will attract only those in the size wanted, where to find them, how to look after them, and what's the best thing to do with them?

11. CUSTOMER VALUE

DIRECT DOLLAR VALUE
STRATEGIC VALUE
LIFETIME VALUE
COST TO ACQUIRE
COST TO RETAIN
GOOD CITIZENSHIP

A customer is worth the amount of good they do for the business – not merely how much profit they bring from a sale.

It is a negative value for the unprofitable or strategically conflicting.

Customer value is also subject to the perspective from which it is being evaluated, with no customer having only one value.

DIRECT DOLLAR VALUE

Fundamentally a relative value – a proportion of total profits for a product or time.

One customer generating ten percent of total gross profit per month has more dollar value than any one of five customers making up ten percent.

It's also a snapshot view, recognising contribution for the period under consideration, not potential growth or strategic value.

STRATEGIC VALUE

The strategic value of a customer is fuel for the next chapter, titled WHAT TO CARRY. The more a customer contributes to chosen strategies – the more value they are.

There are strategic values within chosen paths and daily operations.

For instance, selling into a market predominately served by a competitor might break down an unspoken agreement to not poach each other's customers. Despite the sale being profitable, the customer has a negative value because it threatens a convenient arrangement.

A non-profitable customer is valuable if key to profitable customers.

For instance, a web designer may provide overly elaborate service for a Chamber of Commerce's site. A customer with little direct profit but hugely valuable as a key to members of the Chamber.

Customer value is also dependant on the life cycle stage of the business.

If production levels are near optimum, a customer's value aligns with the profit on each transaction. But, if an increase in output is needed, a customer's potential has more influence on their value.

Customers purchasing all they need of what is available to them don't have much expansion potential. Customers buying only a portion of their needs has strategic value in their potential to increase.

LIFETIME VALUE

Repeat customers have a lifetime value; essentially, the direct dollar value over the time they remain a customer.

This value drives the consideration given to individual customers. In customer versus business conflicts, it provides a measurable dimension – keep the sale? keep the customer?

Lifetime value dictates the maximum amount to spend to get each new customer – see later section of Cost to Acquire.

This approach assumes one customer won't affect overheads (because service capacity is usually in wide bands).

A city-centre coffee shop may estimate the average regular early morning customer remains a customer for three years. Buying coffee two hundred and twenty times per year, with a gross profit of $2.50 per sale, means they are worth $1,650 in additional gross profit.

The lifecycle stage of customers influences their lifetime value; a younger teen has more potential value for a teens-fashion outlet than an older teen.

The lifetime value of customers is central to planning for acquiring and retaining customers.

COST TO ACQUIRE

Word of mouth referrals from other customers, trade associates, family, and friends may look like there has been no dedicated effort to acquire them, but this is rarely the case.

Businesses spend time, effort, and expense during daily operations, creating an environment that fosters referrals.

Face-to-face operations pay more for premises with exposure and location that attracts new customers.

So, the action is not always visible, and costs are not always directly identifiable, but a portion of operating costs wouldn't exist if acquiring customers was not an objective.

For customer acquisition campaigns, the critical issue is not the total cost; it's the cost per new customer.

For example, a city-based business identifies five potential customers in a regional district they might attract with an offer of city prices and free overnight delivery. A road trip costing $700 to call on all five resulting in getting two, meaning the campaign has cost $350 per new customer.

In contrast, a new-customer offer, advertised through social media, will be wasted on almost all the recipients but, at virtually no cost, is regarded as successful if it got one new customer.

The cost of a new customer campaign includes the money spent and any income given away as part of the deal.

Completely giving away income is a powerful approach to connecting with new customers and breaking their existing buying patterns.

A new fast-food shop could give a free burger to anyone entering in the first week. The loss of revenue (on burgers) saves advertising costs, and the staff and overheads would have been under-utilised in that first week.

The sooner customers are on board, the sooner the shop makes money from them. So, although existing exposure and promotions will eventually attract enough customers, there is an advantage in accelerating that take-up.

Acceleration is particularly relevant for start-ups, especially those with substantial fixed operating costs incurring from day one.

Estimating the lifetime value of the targeted customers is crucial in working out the maximum amount it is worth spending to get each new one.

COST TO RETAIN

To retain customers, a business's best friend is the absence of bad rather than the presence of good.

By their nature or by their chosen image, some businesses project a constant state of excitement. But, in the main, commerce is conducted in a calm and considered manner. If nothing goes wrong, the customer is not constantly thinking about changing.

Operating standards are significant in keeping customers, and a portion of the costs of maintaining those standards is therefore attributable to retaining customers.

Needs and wants: there is a subtle but essential difference between what a customer needs and what they want. Customers commonly want more than the operator thinks they need.

Unless it has an absolute monopoly, it can't avoid moving from the cheaper operating standard of meeting customer needs to the dearer standard of meeting customer wants.

Few customers don't regard price as a significant factor in buying decisions. There are customers, and products or services, where price is the only reason for using a particular supplier.

Therefore, it is essential to maintain an acceptable pricing level regardless of the cost in terms of loss of greater profits.

The costs of loyalty freebies and give-aways are usually not separated in financial reports; nonetheless they are a direct cost of retaining customers and an important element in evaluating the value of a customer.

Maintaining cutting-edge product or subject knowledge is critical to attracting and retaining customers in many industries and professions.

The cost of maintaining high standards of knowledge is clear to see for direct costs and time spent on seminars, webinars, subscriptions etc.

Costs not so obvious or separately identifiable are time spent with suppliers to learn more and sharing that knowledge with customers.

Realistically assessing the costs of retaining customers gives a better view of the value of each customer.

GOOD CITIZENSHIP

A business is not a thing with its own set of altruistic, charitable, sport, or moral motivations; these are the province of the owners.

The owners make the decisions to promote a good citizen image, and they do it for financial success, usually by attracting and retaining customers.

Like all decisions, it comes down to cost versus benefit.

It is straightforward to identify the direct costs of good citizenship, especially when it's as distinct as painting 'save the forest' on vehicles. But indirect costs (like vehicle downtime for signwriting) are difficult to quantify.

Take the example of a service station in a district that suffers a terrible bushfire; it advertises that, for the next month, ten cents per litre of fuel sold will go to the bushfire relief fund.

Costs are the advertising, the ten cents per litre of profit given away, and indirect costs in administering the campaign.

Such a campaign relies on increased sales, with profit on the additional litres sold (after the ten-cent donation) helping to offset campaign costs.

The overall result may be an excellent citizenship image, giving long term loyalty value at relatively little cost.

The sincerity and desire of the owners to help the tragic consequences of the fire are not in question, but it is a business decision to do it through the service station.

Knowing the strategic or financial value of customers is essential to managing directions and operating levels.

Knowing the lifetime value sets measurable expenditure limits on the cost to acquire each new customer – sums that appear excessive become realistic compared to a customer's worth.

12. PRODUCTS TO CARRY

CORE PRODUCTS

PHYSICAL LIMITATIONS

FINANCIAL ASPECTS

TARGETED CUSTOMERS

PRODUCT BY RELATIONSHIP

SELF-SABOTAGE

EASIEST

PRODUCT LIFE CYCLE

WHEN TO BIN IT

WHEN TO STOP CARRYING IT

TABLE

How to balance what to carry with what the market will buy?

'Will buy' is key. What the customer wants, or needs, can be different to what they will buy.

What is wanted is important but having everything every customer wants wouldn't necessarily make the business successful.

It may not have the exact brand, colour, size, quantity, etc. a customer wants, but if it is within the market they are serving, they at least need an acceptable alternative.

The more fundamental the products are to the market, the more exact the products need to be.

CORE PRODUCTS

A major driver of the products to carry is explainable by the concept of 'core' and 'non-core' products.

A core product is one that is essential to serve and keep the targeted market. Not carrying a core item means sending customers to competitors to get the missing items and risk losing other sales.

For instance, an electrical appliance store in a developing suburb loses customers if it doesn't have core household appliances such as fridges, washing machines, stoves, heaters, kitchen appliances, and vacuum cleaners.

A non-core product is one the chosen market segments presents the opportunity to sell, but not the absolute necessity.

Generally, non-core are items customers don't rely on that business to supply. It will therefore not suffer too much loyalty loss if they don't carry them.

For example, the electrical appliance store carrying non-core products such as gas barbeques and outdoor settings or personal appliances such as shavers and hair dryers.

PHYSICAL LIMITATIONS

A small inner-suburban shop selling decorative plants, pots and garden supplies is an excellent demonstration of the physical limitations of premises.

Its core market is small gardens, apartment patios, and indoor plants; the shop is covered floor to ceiling with products serving only those markets. Displays of pipes, associated fittings and heavy-duty tools needed to service sizable projects get left to other suppliers.

Products have physical limitations. Perishable products become problematic when gaps between supply availability are longer than the shelf life of the product. Partnering these with products with opposite supply patterns provides a continuous solution to the market's needs.

An example of partnering perishable products with intermittent supply is foliage plants used by florists in flower arrangements. Plants only seasonally available get partnered with others, also only seasonal available but with different timings, to create a continuous solution.

Physical limitations also come about by staff and equipment capacities. For instance, if it takes two people to deliver a stock item and only one person is available most of the time.

Physical limitations, by premises, the nature of the product, staff, and equipment, are tolerable for non-core items but highly damaging when it affects core products and services.

FINANCIAL ASPECTS

If there is a choice of suppliers for a product, direct cost is not the only financial consideration in choosing which to use.

For instance, the cheapest costs can come from importing the goods, but it requires several months forward ordering, sizable quantities, with payment on delivery.

Per-unit it is a cheap option, but despite this, the choice may be to buy in smaller quantities locally with 7-day delivery and 30-day payment terms.

Cheaper per-unit costs that come at the expense of greater financial risk, earlier cash outlay, and higher inventory levels are not always the best choice.

For price-sensitive core products these negatives are a necessary cost.

TARGETED CUSTOMERS

It is financially and physically impossible to carry everything every possible customer wants; the objective is to have products that satisfy 'enough' customers.

It is a matter of identifying the customers wanted, and the markets that yield them, as primary targets.

Next, decide which goods those customers:
- Fully expect to be able to purchase.
- Half expect to purchase.
- May buy if they happen to see them.

That is, the core products and varying degrees of non-core products for each targeted market segment.

Targeting specific and well-defined market segments as primary targets doesn't exclude secondary markets; they simply don't get the same priority to resources.

The more each market segment is understood, the easier it is to know when to carry more than one brand and quality, what product sizes and packaged quantities to have, and the extent of associated and support products.

PRODUCT BY RELATIONSHIP

Some product relationships evolve from obvious associations; anyone selling car tyres also considers carrying tubes, valves, tyre repair kits, car jacks, and wheels.

Delving deeper, the tyre seller considers carrying those same products for recreational vehicles, performance cars, trucks, farm equipment, forklifts, mobile equipment, wheelbarrows, motorcycles, and bicycles.

The answer to knowing where to stop and where to expand is absolutely based on targeted customers.

Another relationship emerges by analysing the customer demographic target market groups.

A shop selling irrigation products might also carry hats, boots, and wet weather gear. Though there is no direct market link between the products, people buying the irrigation gear are also be in the market for these items.

An auto parts retailer targeting the high-performance sector will carry more car-branded jackets and caps than one targeting the commercial fleet market.

SELF-SABOTAGE

Operators sabotage their profit by carrying two products that serve the same need in the same market segment. This remains true despite both being individually sufficiently profitable to carry.

Take the example of a café selling a range of cookies from large jars on the counter alongside a range of proprietary chocolate and confectionery bars. Both lines target impulse buys from the takeaway trade, and both are in the same spending bracket.

However, though the proprietary ranges are sufficiently profitable to justify carrying, the cookies are twice as profitable. All things being equal, the same numbers of sales would happen if only cookies were there.

So, each time the café sells a proprietary snack instead of a cookie, they make less profit without increasing customer satisfaction.

Selling two products serving the same customer need in a non-core range is only justified when the combined profit from both is greater than the profit from only one.

EASIEST

When there is a choice between similar products, a decision on which to carry comes down to the ease of holding, displaying, and handling.

For instance, the tyre seller may have two suppliers with a range of valve cores. One comes in cardboard boxes and needs to be ordered six at a time for each size. The other comes in individual blister packs along with a wall-mounted display rack the sales rep replenishes on each visit.

Clearly, the second range is the one to carry. It is such a low-value item its smaller margin doesn't significantly affect profits, and the price is not challenging the customers.

PRODUCT LIFE CYCLE

The life cycle of an individual core product is not an important consideration because its inclusion is essential anyway - to serve the core market.

Non-core items are another matter entirely.

Non-core products, at an introductory stage, offer the chance to get in on the ground floor and gain a valuable new market segment.

If the non-core product is already well accepted and shows indications of being saleable for many years, it adds immediate strength and balance to the overall product mix.

For the others, adding uncertainty for a non-core product is only worthwhile for the chance of decent returns. Usually, the future is not dependant on the success of non-core products, so more risks and experimentation are acceptable.

A product in the declining stage of its life cycle promises a declining rate of profitability. The challenge is to predict the rate of decline to establish whether anticipated lifetime profits justify the initial and ongoing carrying costs.

WHEN TO BIN IT

Binning an existing item means facing up to waste that already exists and removing it from inventory.

Social issues and personal dislikes of wastage come into play after recognising waste, not in recognising whether it is waste.

Perishable goods wilt, rot, smell, look terrible and generally drive customers away. Non-perishable items become unsaleable by manufacturing defects, customer interference, poor handling, terrible display conditions, and a myriad of other reasons.

But how they became unsaleable doesn't matter:

- They are taking up space a saleable item could be occupying.
- Their continued display is presenting a poor image.
- Customers aren't getting what they want.

It's not how much they initially cost or what a shame it is to throw them out; it's all about the costs of continuing to hold them.

Keeping it and not selling it is no different than binning it, except it costs more.

WHEN TO STOP CARRYING IT

A decision to stop carrying an item is not about scrapping what is there; it's about not re-ordering it; removing it from the list of things usually carried.

Display and storage space is precious; using it to hold items that are never going to sell or take so long to sell that the cost of holding them is more than they sell for, is wasting it.

When needing more shelving or floor space, deleting a range of slow-moving non-core products is a cheap means of increasing the available space.

Suppose the tyre seller recognised only a low-profit market segment was buying motorcycle tyres. In that case, they stop catering for them, freeing up the space from motorcycle-specific inventory, racks, and hoists.

Future profits from losing that market segment will be less than the cost of other ways to accommodate more profitable products.

Later chapters, on inventory and working capital, look at decisions affecting individual items.

TABLE

WHAT TO CARRY

		Product category	
		Core	**Non-core**
Customer category	**Primary**	Inventory priority: **Essential** Price sensitivity: **High** (at total package level) Customer expectation: **Absolute**	Inventory priority: **Desirable** Price sensitivity: **Medium** Customer expectation: **Convenience**
	Secondary	Inventory priority: **Desirable** Price sensitivity: **Medium** Customer expectation: **Convenience**	Inventory priority: **Optional** Price sensitivity: **High** Customer expectation: **No priority**

Deciding what to carry means identifying the target market and clarifying how extensively to meet their requirements.

It is impossible to service all customers fully; the choice comes down to which to service more fully than others.

13. OFFERING SERVICES

EMPLOYEE HOURLY COSTS

SELF-EMPLOYED CONTRACTORS

INCIDENTAL

PROVIDING USE

The market drives the price achievable - the same as it does for products.

Targeting customers, markets, finance, and operating strategies, as covered in the previous chapter on products, are adaptable to services.

What is distinctly different for services is that their cost is rarely as clear as for products.

Where labour is the primary component, the costs can be estimated reasonably accurately. Other cases need a global approach, matching total annual costs, recovery units, and achievable prices.

Generally, the ability to allocate direct costs varies according to whether the service's role is:

- **Primary:** Providing personal service is the primary reason for existence. (Tradies, professionals, healthcare workers, and entertainers.)
- **Joint:** Contract work, or in conjunction with the provision of equipment or premises. (Transport, builders, taxi drivers, concerts, and motels.)
- **Incidental:** Provided to support the sale of products. (product warranty repairs, key cutting, and wheel balancing for a tyre seller.)

The following topics deal principally with calculating profitability - for individual services where possible and globally where it's not.

EMPLOYEE HOURLY COSTS

When employees perform the service, it is critical to know how much it costs to make them available, and this is always far more than the direct hourly pay rate!

Although elements vary between occupations, workplaces, and contract conditions, there are two fundamental lines of approach to calculating the cost:

Total cost of the employee: Total annual wages are only the beginning; the on-costs take some extracting.

On-costs include superannuation, workers compensation, uniforms & PPE, certifications, and any cost directly attributable to having an extra person employed.

Recovery base: This is the number of hours or units of service the cost is recoverable over (chargeable hours) over a year.

It is impossible to allocate all of an employee's paid hours to a job; the employee isn't even at work for such paid time as annual leave, long service leave, public holidays, and personal leave.

Not all hours an employee is present at work can are chargeable to a job. There can be unfillable gaps in demand during the day, non-chargeable travel and set-up time, training, and research time.

Therefore: The cost of making a person available is the total annual cost of the employee divided by the number of hours (or units of work) directly allocated to jobs during that year.

There are often industry estimates for employee on-costs, cited as, for example, 60% on-costs (160% of the employee's base hourly rate).

SELF-EMPLOYED CONTRACTORS

Tradies, professionals and others with valuable skills.

For instance, housing construction functions on tradies operating on their own, then there are professions, the IT industry, and consultants of every persuasion.

And, usually, each contractor has little control over their charge rate.

But regardless of occupation, whether the charge for a service is a standard hourly or daily rate, estimating if the rate on offer is satisfactory is relatively straightforward.

The approach parallels calculating employee hourly costs, it is:

- What are the operators overall annual costs of being in business?
- How much profit is wanted?
- How many hours/days will be chargeable?
- Then, total the costs and profit wanted, and divide it by the number of chargeable days or hours per year.

Costs for a carpenter include their vehicle (depreciation and running costs), equipment replacement, communications, sickness and accident insurance, and tax compliance.

For a bookkeeper, costs include maintaining an office, IT expenses, communications, advertising, and insurance.

Profit wanted is subjective but principally would be the total income possible as an employee, plus extra for the risks and insecurity of being self-employed.

Estimating chargeable days takes into account days not intended to work on (weekends and holidays) and days not able to be worked on (wet days and downtime through hold-ups).

Estimates also need to consider any non-chargeable time quoting, travelling, and sourcing materials.

INCIDENTAL

Despite generating revenue, a service may be more for strategic purposes than direct profit; the amount recovered for it set by its relationship with an image or product.

A kitchen goods retailer servicing the catering industry is obliged to offer knife sharpening services. The price charged will be consistent with their competitors, whether it can be done in-store, by existing staff, in idle time, or contracted out at a much greater cost.

Incidental services also arise from opportunities associated with the business type.

For instance, a furniture retailer may offer interior decoration services targeted at commercial buyers.

When providing the service is motivated by opportunity rather than necessity, it needs to generate realistic profits.

PROVIDING USE

Services are not all about doing something; they include making something available. Car hire, venue admittance, tennis court hire, and accommodation are examples.

In these situations, the direct costs per use are entirely invisible. Still, the same principles of total annual cost divided by the expected number of recovery units will estimate the cost per use.

Adding the desired income to the costs, before dividing by the recovery units, gives an estimate of the lowest acceptable price.

With less identifiable direct costs than products, choosing which services to provide takes whole-of-year calculations to determine what is acceptable.

14. PRICING

COST DOESN'T MATTER
PRICE VERSUS SERVICE
LEADING PRICES
MONOPOLY PRICING
TEMPORARY FLUCTUATIONS
MANIPULATING SALES PATTERNS
SLOW-MOVING ITEMS

Price-setting decisions are driven by such considerations as the:

- Selling prices of alternative products
- Perceived value of similar products.
- Market image
- Location; especially for bricks and mortar outlets

For new or truly unique products and services, the pricing contest is also against what people need to stop spending on to start spending on this.

Also, it is not merely whether a product sells, but how many sell. In almost all cases, the higher the price, the less that sell.

Pricing is a battle with infinite combinations of constantly changing elements with no measure of victory, only outcome. For whatever success is achieved and measured, there is no measure for the success that different pricing would have achieved.

COST DOESN'T MATTER

Of course, cost matters, but it has no relevance to what a customer is prepared to pay for the product or service.

Customers care about what it is worth to them and how much it is elsewhere, not what it cost to make it available.

Businesses focus on the difference between cost and selling price; the gap between those two points determines if the item is worth selling.

It is common for retailers to add a standard profit margin to their buying price to set a price, leading to a misconception that cost is setting the selling price.

Standard markups result in prices the market accepts because the wholesaler/manufacturer/importer has anticipated those markups in setting their selling price to the retailer.

Even for regular products, when a once-only chance to buy at a much lower price arises, the standard markup gets abandoned in favour of continuing to sell at the regular price and making extra profit.

Applying a standard markup to products that don't have established cost and selling prices, is gambling - the resulting price could be more or less than the best acceptable price.

If it's over-priced, it won't sell well; if it's under-priced, it sells extra well, losing potential profit.

PRICE VERSUS SERVICE

When comparing prices, it is essential to establish the level of service accompanying each of those prices.

Products that are elements of a larger sale and not something bought regularly are more sensitive to service than price.

Price has almost no influence when the sums of money are a minor part of a larger project.

When purchasing an overseas trip through an agent, the focus is on destination and travel alternatives. Less attention goes to the cost of visa application services, travel insurance, and airport transfers, and usually, their prices are less keen than the main ticket items.

This scenario is typical for once-off buyers of technical items and DIY projects. Service and advice are most important, meaning any service-oriented business pricing secondary components as if they're selling competitively, is passing up profit needlessly.

Typically, primary products will be priced as low as it takes to attract customers, and the prices of secondary products are at recommended retail.

LEADING PRICES

When most products have standard industry prices, a business may deliberately drop the price on a highly visible item to differentiate itself from competitors.

A building supplies retailer may keep bagged cement prices low because it is an item that is purchased in the early stages of a project. Led by the low cement price, customers accept the store as pricing competitively and give it more opportunities to supply other materials during the remainder of the project.

Bakeries sell coffee to attract customers to their baked goods. They, therefore, sell their coffee at a low price to draw 'coffee and cake' customers from the coffee shops.

This strategy has a narrow range of applications and risks a reduced gross margin for no advantage. Lowering the price can increase sales only of those products, with no flow-on to the rest of the range.

Revisiting the earlier examples: if the building supplier dropped the price of door fittings instead of cement, the customer probably wouldn't know about it until the project was almost finished.

If there is no nearby coffee shop, the bakery is unlikely to make enough profit from the few extra customers to cover the reduced profit on the coffees they would have sold anyway.

MONOPOLY PRICING

A product so unique it doesn't sell against any existing thing in the market, yet is in solid demand, has a wide range of possible pricing points. Price setting, in this monopoly situation, requires a conscious look at long-term sales implications.

If the aim is to capture the entire market for a long time, the strategy is to price low enough to make it less attractive for competitors to gear up and get into the market.

In a short-term monopoly position, the strategy may be to price higher and reap as much profit as possible while it exists.

The choice is to either set lower prices to make moderate profits for a long time, or higher prices to make greater profits for a short time.

TEMPORARY FLUCTUATIONS

Fluctuations in the context of temporary rises and falls in the cost of goods and or the supply of goods, not long-term changes.

Existing businesses have already structured for predictable changes, and the market accepts those predictable supply or price variations.

For fledgling businesses and for abnormal temporary changes in the cost or supply of goods, operators assess:

- The effect on gross margin from not changing the selling price.
- The need to review current inventory carrying and re-order levels.
- The availability of enough display and storage space when the volume is increasing.
- Better temporary use of the existing display and storage space when volume drops.
- The new (temporary) price versus volume balance for the highest profit.
- The price and volume levels that give the best customer loyalty.
- Customer sentiment if there is even a hint of price gouging.

Fluctuating prices are normal in many occupations, particularly retail outlets and those dealing with natural produce; as a result, customers are generally well informed and accepting of variations.

Customers are also unforgiving of opportunism and quick to take advantage of under-pricing.

MANIPULATING SALES PATTERNS

Prices are adjusted amongst products and services to steer sales in directions that work best.

Sales patterns will be manipulated by prices when comparable products have different profitability.

An example is a café pricing their labour-intensive pure fruit juice drinks at the higher end of the acceptable price range. While offering all that customers expect, they are not encouraging more than necessary away from the more profitable coffee sales.

When there is a preference to deal with one supplier over others, the preferred supplier's products get priced more competitively. And this is not necessarily by reducing their price; it more probably is from increasing the prices of the less favoured suppliers.

An end-of-line run-out sale is price manipulation in action. Reducing the price of discontinuing lines swings a larger portion of sales to those products to clear the last of them.

SLOW-MOVING ITEMS

It doesn't matter whether many or few of a product sell; it only matters that each product trades at sufficient benefit to the business.

So, the term 'slow moving' is either a measure against expectation – not selling as many as expected, or a statement about comparative profitability – not making as much profit as an alternate item.

Slow movers come about when the product is well outside what the customers expect to see on a site or in the premises; in other words, that product was not part of the reason they entered.

Obsolescence and product redundancy also erode sales until a product sells fewer than present display space and promotion warrants.

Whatever the origin of slow-moving items, their profit margin needs to increase, or the expense of carrying them reduced, until they are no longer a disadvantage.

An example of non-core slow-moving products is a specialist truck tyre supplier carrying a range of small vehicle tyres to service customers' support vehicles. The small tyres are not drawing customers, so they are not discounted, and the extra margin helps compensate for their low sale volumes.

Pricing is a powerful weapon: it influences which products sell, how many sell, and management effort.

Businesses in price-competitive markets constantly review both their overall pricing policies and individual product prices.

15. TURNOVER

Useful uses
Analysing it
Transaction costs

Three financial terms constantly bandied about are: turnover, gross profit, and net profit; this chapter, and the next two, explain their make-up and use.

Turnover, gross sales, total sales, billings, daily take, or whatever it's called, is the most visible, definable, easiest to extract, and most likely to mislead.

Turnover measures what has sold, but any use of turnover to indicate profit is full of risk. There are so many things that affect the figures making it up, and the costs associated with it, that its profitability changes dramatically from period to period.

Turnover and productivity are also not fully aligned. For instance, the daily turnover by a taxi driver gives a valuable measure of productivity because the driver bills all jobs for the day with no carry-overs. Therefore, daily turnover equates to daily productivity.

On the other hand, a steel fabricator spending two weeks on an order has no turnover for that time despite being productive. The enormous turnover on the day of billing doesn't in any way represent that day's productivity. (Neither figure indicates profit.)

For bookkeeping and profit reporting, turnover doesn't include GST charged on sales. Accounting packages and point-of-sale systems usually reflect this by reporting GST as a non-turnover portion of receipts.

Sales figures that include GST still give a quick and easy daily trading comparison (especially for the taxi driver). Generally, though, the only value of this combined figure is for use in cash flow calculations.

USEFUL USES

Turnover helps interpret market movements. For example, comparing a period (week, month, year, etc.) to equivalent previous periods shows market trends and marketing strategies and service delivery effectiveness.

Past daily turnover figures are a valuable predictor of turnover and, therefore, staffing requirements; essential when employing staff on casual rates.

Turnover, broken down into products and departments, indicates performance and stress on staff and other resources. It is also a guide for direction in production and inventory investment.

Turnover per employee is an indication of effectiveness in delivering sales; useful for increasing hours for the more effective and giving more training or supervision to the less effective.

ANALYSING IT

The more turnover is broken into sub-categories, the more valuable comparisons become.

Valuable patterns emerge from breaking invoices and till records into categories of customer, invoicing unit used, the employee processing the sale, products sold, time, and payment method.

Sales software modules have pre-set reports, with flexibility on presentation, allowing a kind of 'pick & mix' approach to matching and grouping categories of turnover.

For instance, a scientific equipment supplier may want to know who their largest customers are, what their total spend of each is, what product groups they are buying; and the amount transacted in-store, by telephone, or online.

The types of data commonly available for this pick & mix approach are:

Dollar value: total for each transaction and each line item on the invoice or till docket.

Customers: whether a customer is retail or commercial; what pricing structure they are on.

Outlet: which store; which counter within the store; taken by telephone; online order.

Employee: whose sign-on was used for the till, pc, or tablet.

Product: identification codes that enable reporting by individual items and the accumulated value of the groups of products and services.

Time: recording the day and time enables report filtering by date range, time of the day, and individual or groups of days.

Payment method: Credit sale; card; cash; direct credit; PayPal; Afterpay; and booking agency.

Turnover is expressible in either dollars or the number of products sold, and the choice varies between business types:

- Retailers use dollars. It is easy to get, instantly available, and divisible into sub-categories to track sales trends and profitability.

- Manufacturers use product numbers. Focusing on the flow of work, the type of product that needs replacing is more immediate value than dollars received.
- Contractors use turnover. Though it is of little value until divided between the charges for materials, direct labour, and the (joint) recovery of overheads and profit.

For day-to-day management, turnover must be instantly available. It becomes a matter of identifying the essential information required, then finding the quickest and cheapest means of getting it with 'enough' accuracy.

TRANSACTION COSTS

An agent, or collection service, may deduct fees from the money they receive and forward on only a net amount. The amount the business gets, therefore, understates the turnover.

For instance, online booking agencies typically deduct their commission from their payments. The proceeds received on settlement from a property developer's sales has agents' commissions, settlement fees, and rates adjustments deducted.

If the party paying the money is not the actual customer, charges deducted from that payment need adding back (the receipt grossed up) to reveal true turnover from customers.

Turnover is a valuable measure of marketing and product strategies, though it is also a poor indicator of profitability.

When used only as an indicative tool, the instant availability of unrefined figures from sales reports is valuable enough to outweigh slight inaccuracies.

16. GROSS PROFIT

COST OF GOODS SOLD
EXPRESSING GP
FICTIONAL GP
VALUE
JUGGLING GP

Gross profit (GP) is the money remaining after deducting the cost of goods sold from the turnover received for them.

At a per-product level, there must be enough dollars in each sale to justify its existence.

Across all sales, the accumulated gross profit expressed in dollars is the only measure of whether it covers operating costs and the profit required.

COST OF GOODS SOLD

For a simple retail situation, it's the cost of the product, the cost of getting it into the store, and any wrapping, packaging, or freight, to deliver to the customer.

Cost of goods sold does not include the costs of having the business exist and operate; costs of owning, staffing, and operating, are overhead costs.

For services and manufacturing, it is the direct costs of what is being sold or provided, plus other processing and operating costs while, and because of, producing that service or product.

For manufactured products, the cost includes raw materials, power and wages directly attributable to the item, power and fuel used to drive the manufacturing tools, packaging and presentation, and any cost to deliver to the customer.

Wastage, tasters, display samples, damage, defects, and unsaleable stock, are a cost of goods sold; though not sold, they are direct consequences of selling.

For instance, if the garden shop lost two punnets of seedlings out of a tray of twelve, the cost of the entire tray remains the cost of the ten that did sell.

Power used by the welder in the steel fabricator's workshop is a cost of goods sold; power used by the welder in their building maintenance workshop is an overhead.

Power used on lighting, air conditioning, turning display stands, lighting neon signs, operating the point-of-sale devices, and controlling the security gate to the carpark, are all overhead costs.

EXPRESSING GP

Gross profit is money, a number of dollars.

It is dollars per individual product, per basket of goods sold, or for all sales over a defined trading period.

GP is commonly given as a percentage, carrying an underlying presumption of the base used - selling price or cost price.

The base used is not always clear or consistent, risking incorrect presumptions and, therefore, a misleading picture.

A wholesaler stating a product has a hundred percent gross profit is probably basing that calculation as a percentage of the cost. The cost to the retailer is $100, who will sell it for $200.

The retailer, however, normally expresses gross profit percentage on selling price. The $100 gross profit equals fifty percent of the $200 selling price.

Both calculations are accurate and relevant in their circumstances, but misunderstanding which base was used is the difference in believing the gross profit is 50% or 100%.

Percentages obscure profitability. 10% gross profit sounds like a poor return against other items at 50%, but if the 10% product sells for $100 and the 50% product sells for $20, they both have the same gross profit.

Determining product profitability means using dollars, not percentages, and then comparing those dollars to the effort to produce, purchase, store, sell and deliver.

FICTIONAL GP

Gross profit percentage on cost, or markup, are two descriptions of the same data; they express the amount of profit made as a percentage of its cost.

But a percentage of a product's cost is purely fictional when no outlay has been made before receiving money from its sale. That is, selling before paying for it.

For instance, an online retail site might take orders and payments simultaneously and then purchase the goods.

Therefore, considering gross profit in terms of a return on outlay is misleading; there hasn't been any outlay. Selling has been cash positive.

This fictional cost applies to individual products, not necessarily the entire range. For example, the local corner store carries a large portion of their inventory well after paying for it, yet sell bread, milk, newspapers, fruit, and flowers before paying for them.

Up-market restaurants target a gross profit of around 400% on cost, a selling price four times greater than the cost of the ingredients, yet at least half those ingredients haven't been paid for when the diner pays the bill.

Gross profit as a percentage of cost is meaningless. Only when given as dollars can the worth of carrying these products, or preparing this dish, be meaningfully assessed.

VALUE

The value of a gross profit is the amount of the gross profit:
- Less the amount of the owners' time this product uses up.
- Less demand on overheads, such as handling, storage, displaying, financing, etc.
- Plus any strategic advantage of carrying it.
- Plus the present availability of idle capacity.
- Less current cash flow pressures.
- Less special needs of the product.
- Less expected difficulties with suppliers, transport, and customers, attaching to the product.

The result is subjective yet still informative when compared to the equally subjective value of alternative products.

For instance, an electronic sales and repair outlet will aim to make at least the same per hour for selling things as they get for repairing them. Spending an hour selling items that produce half as much in total gross profit as repair work earns in that same hour is pointless.

Valuing gross profit as above may reveal to a café operator they make $2.00 gross profit for the minute and a half to take the order, make, and deliver a coffee. For only another ten seconds of effort, they could pick up a further $1.50 gross profit for selling a muffin.

Being aware of how much gross profit each product and each sale makes provokes valuable management insights.

JUGGLING GP

Pricing positions are set within a range that the market will accept – that is, there is often more than one acceptable price.

Mostly, fewer products sell when pricing is at the higher end of that range and more at the lower end.

The question becomes whether there is a bigger profit for selling more products at a lower GP, or less at a higher GP.

The following table demonstrates, at various GP rates, how far sales volumes could fall after a price rise before the total actual gross profit went down.

* For instance, in the first line, it shows if a business with a 20% GP on sales raised prices by 10%, they can sell 33% fewer products and still make the same gross profit (in dollars).

VOLUME REDUCTION FOR SAME PROFIT

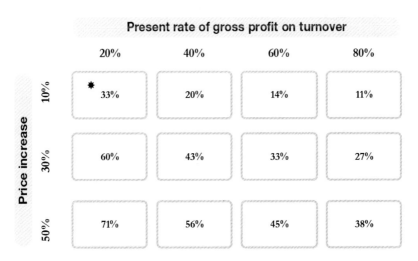

	Present rate of gross profit on turnover			
	20%	40%	60%	80%
10%	✱ 33%	20%	14%	11%
30%	60%	43%	33%	27%
50%	71%	56%	45%	38%

Price increase

The pricing point is a critical marketing issue, with the resulting volumes affecting space needed, staffing, production capacity, and time spent. Yet, it is possible to juggle the price to get the same (existing) total GP on lower sales and therefore less of those elements.

Gross profit measures how much a sale, or group of sales, contributes towards overheads and net profit.

Expressing it as a percentage of turnover helps make instant comparisons between groups of transactions or products.

But gross profit is money, so money is the primary measure of how worthwhile a gross profit is.

17. NET PROFIT

OVERHEADS

LEVERAGING NP WITH PRICES

DRAWINGS

AVAILABILITY

Net profit[6] is what's left after deducting all costs from all turnover for a defined period. It's a whole-of-business measure.

Net profit is a financial measure. It shows how much money the invested capital, the risks taken, and the time and effort expended has produced for the owners.

No measure is more important because it is the primary reason for being in business.

It is valuable for projecting idea outcomes and weighing up and comparing businesses.

It is a big-picture measure that has little use in daily management decisions that focus more on finetuning the elements making it up.

---

[6] The terms net profit and net income get used to describe the same figures. Though there is some difference for public companies, distinction between the two is otherwise meaningless; this chapter uses only net profit.

Sequentially, turnover minus cost of goods sold gives the gross profit; gross profit minus overheads gives the net profit.

OVERHEADS

Overheads are the costs of being in a position to acquire, produce, sell, and provide things.

Included are such things as the cost of accommodation (rent, power, rates, etc.), employee costs (wages, superannuation, workers compensation, etc.), advertising and promotions, insurances, IT, accounting, and maintenance.

Even while not producing or selling anything, overheads continue.

Future chapters provide discussion on individual overheads, so no in-depth look is warranted in this section.

LEVERAGING NP WITH PRICES

Even small changes in price, without a corresponding change in costs, have a vastly greater effect on net profit.

For instance, selling ten items that cost four dollars each, for five dollars each, produces a turnover of fifty dollars and a gross profit of twenty.

Selling the same items for six dollars produces a sixty-dollar turnover with a gross profit of thirty, with no increase in costs. Increasing the price by one-fifth gives one and a half times the profit.

It doesn't stop there. Overheads won't change, meaning the net profit increases by the same amount as the gross profit. Net profits are massively smaller than gross profits, so the increase has a far more significant effect.

The following table demonstrates that leveraging effect on a takeaway café turning over one million dollars a year for a net profit of one hundred thousand dollars.

They have failed to raise prices in line with competitors, and the opportunity now is to increase all prices by five percent, with no extra costs of goods, no additional overheads, and no loss in turnover.

LEVERAGING NET PROFIT ON PRICES

	Current position		5% Price rise		% 'age increase
			Increase	New amount	
Turnover	$1,000,000	100%	$50,000	$1,050,000	5%
Less: Cost of goods sold	$400,000	40%	$0	$400,000	0%
Gross Profit	$600,000	60%	$50,000	$650,000	8%
Less: Overheads	$500,000	50%	$0	$500,000	0%
Net Profit	$100,000	10%	$50,000	$150,000	50%

It is simple to feel a 5% increase in prices wouldn't justify the angst of managing the push-back from regular customers, but the reality is vastly different.

Net profit increases from $100,000 to $150,000, that is, almost a thousand dollars a week, for no additional effort.

It shows how good a move the price rise is, but it also demonstrates how much the failure to keep prices up to the market is costing.

DRAWINGS

Drawings is the term for money used for non-business purposes.

When owners take money to make personal payments, it does not change the net profit, only the funds remaining for business purposes.

Calling a regular fortnightly payment to an owner, wages[7], regardless of fairness or justification, is a fictional use of the word.

Regular drawings approximating a wage at least serve as a test on the profitability and management - if the payment is unsustainable, the business is not making the income or cash flow required.

Making home loan repayments from the business bank account is drawings, as is the personal portion of motor vehicle costs, and paying the owners' income tax.

AVAILABILITY

A $150k net profit does not reflect as $150k extra in the bank account.

Profits get disbursed in ways including:

- Drawings: as per the previous section.
- Debt reduction: paying down loans.
- Asset acquisition: purchasing assets from existing funds instead of additional capital contributions or borrowings.
- Reducing working capital: decreasing the overdraft, increasing accounts receivable, decreasing accounts payable, or increasing inventory.

---

[7] Businesses operated through an incorporated company can make payments to the owners recognised as wages for legal and taxation purposes. These reduce the profit and, therefore, the income otherwise distributed to the owner. Total income, or loss, remains the same regardless of how it is structured to pass to the owners.

- Growth: Growth creates a need for more working capital, and the primary source of increased working capital is net profit.

The share of the net profit available for discretionary spending depends on the growth stage, capital commitments, and funds management.

> *Net profit is a measure of the overall financial result over a specific time.*
>
> *It encourages reflection on past alternatives chosen and guides future direction.*

18. INVENTORY

PRODUCTS OFFERED
INVENTORY SOFTWARE
OPTIMAL LEVEL
RE-ORDER QUANTITY
RE-ORDER POINT
WHICH SUPPLIER
STOCK ROTATION
STOCK TURNS
COST OF HOLDING
VALUING INVENTORY

Inventory is anything on hand to sell.

For a retailer, it is products purchased to sell and not yet sold.

For a manufacturer, it's all the raw materials, outsourced components on hand, partly manufactured goods, and completed goods.

For assemblers of products, such as custom IT hardware, heavy equipment suppliers, or food hamper suppliers, it's any item on hand intended to form part of a future sale.

For an online business that charges for delivery, it includes prepaid parcel delivery packages held ready for use.

Inventory does not include items made unsaleable because of their incorporation into promotional displays. Nor does it include unsaleable goods not yet discarded.

Inventory doesn't include items on hand to sell but not owned by the business.

For instance, a clothing range on consignment to a fashion outlet; ownership remains with the consignor until sold or returned. Also, artworks held by a gallery for sale on commission are not the inventory of the gallery.

It doesn't need to be on the business's premises or under its direct control. Seasonal raw materials purchased but only drawn from the supplier's warehouse as required is still inventory.

Clothing on consignment in the fashion store is not inventory of the store; it is inventory of the party putting it there and remains so until either sold or returned.

Damaged inventory becomes less valuable or less in demand, but it remains inventory when there is an intention to sell it.

PRODUCTS OFFERED

Products offered for sale, and inventory, are not necessarily the same thing.

Stores often carry a fraction of what they offer, then take orders for quantities, and products, not on hand.

For instance, a plumbing goods supplier has only a few of the most basic and universally used products in their inventory. They then display a sample of fixtures and fittings and provide brochures and advice to cover a far more comprehensive range.

Others operate under a model of only offering what they already own; this includes salvage yards, retailers of distributors' end-of-line products, clothing shops, mobile food vans, jewellers, and supermarkets.

INVENTORY SOFTWARE

Few retailers operate without a computerised inventory system. Usually, it links with other modules such as a point-of-sale invoicing and receipting system, accounts payable, and the general ledger.

Manufacturers may have industry-specific inventory systems that manage production schedules, track materials, components, and finished products from raw materials to the completed and packaged goods in the retail space.

Fast food outlets may consider inventory systems as little than for generators of daily supply orders.

At their core, inventory management systems record the quantity of each product available for sale and report the total cost of inventory currently held. For products carried continuously, their most critical daily function is generating re-order lists.

Three key drivers of inventory management are:
- Optimum level.
- Re-order quantity.
- Re-order point.

The following three sections expand on these drivers.

OPTIMAL LEVEL

The optimal level is the number of products to which the system attempts to re-build individual lines.

It is a nominal number - a quantity that might never be on hand. It needs to be high enough to ensure sales between raising the order and restocking the shelves don't reduce the number on hand below an acceptable level.

For some products and markets, the optimal level fluctuates with seasons, holidays, or even on days of the week.

Businesses with large seasonal fluctuations in sale volumes that set-and-forget their optimal number risk having more on hand than they need most of the time, then not enough at critical times.

For products never to be re-ordered, the optimal number has no relevance.

RE-ORDER QUANTITY

This is the number of products usually ordered, usually a pre-set quantity, such as three units, one carton, 100 kilograms, etc.

Re-order quantities take into account how frequently orders are possible, packaging sizes, price differences for broken and full packages, and quantity-pricing brackets.

If the nature of the product dictates the order quantity, the supplier, or supply conditions, further consideration is unnecessary. Any inflexibility gets factored into the re-order point and optimal levels.

RE-ORDER POINT

The re-order point is the lowest number of products a product line can drop to before triggering an order.

Issues to be considered in arriving at the re-order point are:
- Optimal number.
- Re-order quantity.
- Expected rate of sale.
- The time between usual ordering opportunities.
- Estimated number of days between ordering and having the products on hand and ready to sell.
- How critical immediate availability of the product is to customers.
- How critical the customers of this product are.

- The quantity per sale this product is normally, and occasionally, sold in.
- The supplier's 'in full and on time' (IFOT) delivery history.
- The probability of receiving unusable products through quality or transit damage issues.

WHICH SUPPLIER

Logically, the supplier is chosen based on availability, cost, payment terms, order quantities, delivery times, supply reliability, product reliability, availability, personal associations, and convenience.

But, except for niche and truly independent businesses, the operator usually has little choice on which supplier to use.

Branded products are often only available from one supplier. Also, carrying the same brand across the range of products is usually expected, which dictates the supplier for associated products.

Availability, geography, or standard industry practice often dictates the supplier of raw materials and manufacturing components.

In franchises, the agreement dictates the supplier for core products and influences choice on other lines.

Businesses purchasing through a buying group (specialist supplier for an industry) get influenced by rebates and pricing structures that reward buying from that group or through associated suppliers.

Customer preferences for brands and styles are a major influence of which supplier to use.

Having one dominant supplier makes dealings easier and creates a shared interest in a continuing profitable relationship. However, it also creates reliance on that supplier maintaining:

- Positive market perception of quality and brand recognition for their goods.
- Their continued existence.
- A preparedness to trade with the business.

When linked intimately with a supplier, it brings more surety of supply, but it also creates reliance on that supplier's fortunes and mercy.

STOCK ROTATION

Stock rotation effort, moving the oldest to the front and the newest to the less accessible position, is a cause of significant handling and storage costs.

Getting larger deliveries less often reduces these costs both in the storeroom and on the shop floor but increases inventory.

Where shelf-life and available space permits a choice, it comes down to balancing higher handling costs against lower inventory levels.

Most often, the choice is to order more often to keep the inventory of each item as low as possible, enabling more lines for the same total investment.

Products subject to incremental updates, such as evolving electronic devices, benefit from high rotation rates by minimising the number of older versions to sell before the market becomes too aware of the existence of updated versions.

STOCK TURNS

This valuable indicator is nothing more than the number of times per year the amount of inventory they currently hold is purchased.

For instance, a business with an annual cost of goods sold of $3m, and a current inventory of $1m, has three stock turns.

Stock turn rates cut through the fog of convenience, emotions, and market pressures to give an objective view of trends in inventory levels.

Monitoring trends highlights when sales unexpectedly increase or reduce, or if inventory rises or falls, without conscious intention.

For instance, if the stock turn rate slows, that is, gets lower (say 3.0 turns down to 2.8 turns), it means there have been fewer sales in proportion to current inventory held.

A slowing stock turn rate raises the need to:

- Identify if it is because of a temporary situation that will resolve itself.
- Look at whether more promotion and attention are needed to get sales back on track.
- Reduce optimal inventory levels to set future inventory levels slightly lower.

Retailers of products relying on impulse or emotive buys (for example, clothing and giftware) are at risk of building up their proportion of slow-moving stock by failed purchasing choices.

As the proportion of slow movers builds, customers browse increasingly fewer new things, making the experience less satisfying, and sales decline.

Stock turn ratios showing a relentlessly slowing rate, combined with a below-industry benchmark, are highlighting this like a beacon!

Industry benchmarks for stock turn ratios provide a valuable guide in reviewing inventory levels and sales results. They also help in estimating inventory levels for business plans.

Computerised inventory systems provide running reports of stock-turn rates for each product enabling ready reviews of the optimal level and re-order quantity.

Stock-turn rates by inventory category reveal a departments', or individual purchasing officers', compliance with rulings on inventory levels.

COST OF HOLDING

The biggest driver of the cost of holding inventory is the total amount of it.

Maintaining a calculated ideal level is essential; above that level increases costs without benefit and being below it loses sales.

Even small departures from ideal have heavy consequences.

For instance, carrying 5% extra of a product with an optimal inventory value of $1,000 gives an insignificant $50 deviation; this tolerance of minor excess carried across all items in a million-dollar inventory costs an additional $50,000.

An approach of carrying the same number of all sizes of each range of products carried, regardless of the individual sales patterns of each size, increases total inventory significantly.

The total cost of inventory held is not the same as the amount of money the owners have invested in it. Not all inventory held has been paid for at any point in time.

Preferencing suppliers that give longer payment terms reduces financing costs.

Where payment is required 30 days from the end of the month, making smaller (stopgap) orders towards the end of the month and deferring the main order until early next month also reduces financing costs.

Having too little inventory is costly, exceptionally so, because of the profits not made. The damage is to both current sales and customer loyalty.

Also, any item that, by its existence, stops the carrying of a higher profit item, is costing the business the difference in the two profits.

VALUING INVENTORY

Financial reports, and general financial management, requires a figure for the total value of inventory.

Usually, the figure used is the actual amount paid for all that is still on hand, as per the inventory software package.

Using only the cost to determine total value is quick and easy, but it conceals value reductions on the old, obsolete, over-stocked, and damaged items.

For daily management, the value of every individual piece of inventory matters.

When surrounded by inventory and dealing with supply, storage and market issues, the only value that matters is how much it is worth right now, where it is and as it is; value is a current measure. History of its cost is meaningless.

So, for management purposes, the value of each item is:

- How much it will sell for (less a realistic gross profit and the costs of storing and selling it).
- Or, if it's lower, the cost of replacing it.

Value is also affected by the interplay between the amount held of each item, the rate at which it loses value over time, and its selling trends - if a line is over-stocked, it drops the value of each item.

The interplay ranges from blatantly apparent for perishable food lines (requiring constant value review) to something more graduated for fashion goods, seasonal items, electronic gadgets, and products moving into slower life cycle stages.

Inventory for a business sale is valued subject to the terms of the sale agreement. Often it starts with the latest actual cost and then builds in conditions to vary that for old, obsolete, over-stocked, or damaged items.

Demand for inventory is unlimited; available funds and space limit the final holding level.

With the total holding limited, management of the lines and numbers held become critical.

Purchasing failures lay inconspicuously as an ever-increasing proportion of slow-moving lines and therefore producing lower net profits than otherwise achievable.

19. WORKING CAPITAL

FINANCING IT
OVERDRAFTS
CREDIT CARDS
PREPAYMENTS
INVENTORY
ACCOUNTS RECEIVABLE
ACCOUNTS PAYABLE
WORK IN PROGRESS

Working capital is the pool of funds used for daily operations.

It's not only money in the bank; it's anything that will convert to money within twelve months in the ordinary course of operations.

It is regarded as an asset and is the net difference between current assets (principally cash, inventory, and accounts receivable) and current liabilities (mostly accounts payable).

Everyday operations use it, but don't use it up. For instance, paying $5k to a supplier makes the bank balance (asset) go down, but so does the accounts payables (liability); the net difference remains the same.

There is usually a reasonably stable and predictable amount of working capital needed.

Changes come about by making profits, incurring losses, repaying long term loans, making capital payments, or taking money out of the business.

FINANCING IT

Financing working capital is problematic as it's not attractive security to lenders. It is difficult to capture and liquidate it in the event of default.

Then again, loan defaults rarely happen when there is still value in the working capital.

Working capital generally comes from three sources:

- Owners' capital contributions.
- Long-term borrowings - for any shortfall between the owners' contribution and the lowest level of working capital required throughout the year.
- Short term loans (overdrafts and credit cards) - for the amount between the lowest and highest levels. – the fluctuating portion.

OVERDRAFTS

Overdrafts are common for funding the fluctuating part of working capital and, as such, constantly vary from not being used at all to being fully drawn.

The unused portion of an overdraft is invisible in the accounts; they show only the current balance. For working capital purposes, it's how much is still available for drawing out that matters.

So, the cash available for working capital when the current bank balance is $15k credit, but there is also an overdraft facility of $100k, is $115k.

Banks calculate interest on the daily balance plus fixed monthly administration charges; basically, borrowers only pay for the amount they have borrowed each day – not how much they're able to borrow.

CREDIT CARDS

It is usual to regard credit cards for personal use, but there are businesses so small and the need for funds so infrequent, they become a viable short-term solution.

Short-term because it is an expensive form of finance when not paying within any interest-free period.

Importantly, credit cards are an established last line of protecting personal, family, and household needs if the business runs into real strife. Their use for business purposes reduces this valuable reserve.

PREPAYMENTS

Prepayments are expenses paid in advance, such as vehicle registrations, insurances, software licences, hardware maintenance contracts, and professional registrations.

Prepayments drop a year's worth of an expense into one month, with capacity needed to pay it before receiving any benefit.

For large sums, short term loans are available, such as ten to twelve-month loans for the annual workers' compensation or professional indemnity insurance premiums.

Timing the prepayments to come due at a time in the year when cash is usually available also eases the strain.

INVENTORY

Inventory usually is the most significant element of working capital, meaning mismanagement causes the most damage.

It is also the most inflexible, with substantial reductions taking a long and gradual effort.

Lower re-order quantities take time to flow through the entire range, and the lower payments to suppliers take time to flow through accounts payable to the bank account.

Inventory reduction by sales is the preferred solution of many retailers. It gives an instant effect from cash sales and a slightly delayed effect from credit sales.

Price-reductions sales have hidden costs:

- Sales that will have happened eventually get brought forward. The loss in gross margin (from the price reduction) is an expensive way to get the money sooner.

- Regular sales of the price-reduced products happen at a lower gross margin for no strategic purpose.

  For instance, a store-wide price reduction of 20% means regular daily sales still happening, now have a 20% lower selling price - probably more like 50% lower gross margin[8].

The reduced gross profit on sales that were not a result of the price reduction is a costly way to fund working capital.

The recorded inventory level is reduced by revaluations and write-offs but do not affect available working capital because they are non-cash events.

Supply disruptions drop inventory levels and have an immediate negative impact by reducing proceeds from sales.

---

[8] If regular daily sales attracted an average 45% GP on sales, each $100 of turnover cost $55 and has a GP of $45. With those sales made at 20% off, the selling price is $80; the cost is still $55, so the GP is $25 (31%) - that's a 56% reduction in GP.

They also have a delayed positive effect on working capital by reducing future payments to suppliers.

ACCOUNTS RECEIVABLE

To clarify the terminology, these are customers from whom money is due - also called 'debtors' when bookkeepers wrote what was owing on the debit side of the ledger.

Accounts receivable are a necessary part of supplying most non-retail customers. There are industry patterns for payment and, combined with each customer's payment history, cash flow from accounts receivable is reasonably predictable.

A business consistently requiring accounts receivable to be paid ahead of usual industry practice is making sales beyond their working capital capacity.

Solution: inject more working capital or slow down credit sales.

ACCOUNTS PAYABLE

Again, to clarify the terminology, these are suppliers waiting for payment. They used to be called creditors, and yes, on the credit side of the ledger!

For working capital purposes, accounts payables include payments due for GST held, tax deducted from salaries, and regular monthly instalments on loans and leases.

To operate smoothly, there is little flexibility in the timing of the payment of accounts payable.

WORK IN PROGRESS

Contractors commit time and materials on a project before billing it out; 'work in progress' is the term to describe the amount outlaid on that unbilled work.

For contractors, timing is critical to controlling work in progress. Contractors are only able to make a claim when the contract states they can.

The ideal is to receive payment from the customer before paying suppliers for the costs included in each claim.

The skill is in planning work schedules to time the purchase of high-value items immediately before claim points.

For manufacturers of their own inventory, the management of work in progress is parallel to inventory management.

Working capital requirements, even allowing for unexpected and unavoidable emergencies, are reasonably predictable.

Shortages happen when used for unfunded expansion, increased personal drawings, profits are down, and from poor management of individual elements.

Not having enough working capital causes unproductive stress.

20. CAPITAL COSTS

CAPITAL ASSETS

CAPITAL PAYMENTS

Accountants, banks, and the Tax Office have classified payments as either capital or expense for so long it is easy to overlook that most capital payments are also expenses.

Purchases classed as capital usually get paid entirely upfront from specifically allocated owner's contribution or external financing. As such, they don't always impact the daily finances, and it's easy to think of them differently from other costs.

For bookkeeping purposes, they show on the Balance Sheet, not as a charge against profits.

Any drop in value takes deliberate action to recognise in the books as a charge against profits. That charge shows as either depreciation[9] or capital write-off.

Although the calculation of depreciation and capital write-offs is a bit subjective, there is nothing subjective about the existence of the expense.

---

[9] Sometimes the reduction in the value of tangible fixed assets is called depreciation, and for intangible fixed assets, it's called amortisation. In this topic, both reductions are called depreciation.

The Tax Office allows claims for capital costs in politically convenient ways or based on broad industry patterns; it is best not to use these figures to estimate true operating expenses.

The following sections look at capital assets and capital payments separately.

CAPITAL ASSETS

Capital assets remain valuable for more than a year and continue to be valuable after being used.

They come in two forms: 'fixed' and 'intangible'.

Fixed assets are almost everything capable of being seen and touched yet not part of working capital, for example, properties, buildings, vehicles, forklifts, shop fittings, machinery, and computer hardware.

Intangibles can't be seen or touched; things like goodwill[10], mineral exploration licences, and IT software.

Assets that don't usually reduce in value, such as land and goodwill, require no attention in the context of this chapter.

Assets that reduce in value need to have that reduction applied against the profits of the years in which that reduction occurs.

For instance, a restaurant that refurbishes its dining room at the cost of $240,000, anticipating needing to do it again in about six years, charges one-sixth of the expense ($40,000) against the profits of each of the next six years.

A business buying a truck for $400k, expecting to sell it in four years for $100k, is looking at a net cost of $300k over those four years. It, therefore, charges $75k against the profits of each year.

Calculating a depreciation amount for a software licence is much more subjective. It has a value that fades over time yet,

---

[10] When a business purchaser pays more than its assets' total net saleable value, the additional amount is called goodwill.

from day one, the only reasonable chance of getting money for it is from an eventual purchaser of the business.

For licences, the solution is to spread the cost over an arbitrary number of years - the calculation taking as a term the number of years it might be before needing to replace or upgrade it.

CAPITAL PAYMENTS

Capital payments facilitate ongoing operations, but they are not recurring annual costs and have no value that can be passed on.

The costs of setting up a business, the travel, research, professional advice, feasibility, and due diligence costs, produce nothing that continues to exist once operations commence. They're also not a cost of ongoing operations. Yet, there would be no operating without them.

The cost of implementing a new software program and transferring data from the old system is not an operating cost, nor does it have a saleable value. (The hardware and software may have a saleable value but not the implementation.)

Paying a neighbouring tenant to vacate and transfer their lease to the business is a capital payment. It allows expansion without relocation, but nothing is purchased and, it isn't an ongoing operational cost.

When the number of years to which the benefit applies is clear, it is customary to spread the capital cost evenly against the profits for each of those years.

When there is no definable period, the expense gets allocated across an (almost) arbitrary number of years.

For example, basing business establishment costs on how many years the business might operate under the original design.

Capital costs won't come to attention from the usual bookkeeping; they need deliberate consideration.

Rates of tax claims, accounting treatments, and lack of understanding cause confusion, but the costs are often substantial and require recognition.

The fundamental consideration is the periods of income against which to apply them.

21. BUDGETS

Standard monthly income and expenditure reports don't show if trading is on course to produce what the owners are hoping for, but budgets do.

A budget is the anticipated annual financial picture, broken into the expected monthly flow of funds for each income and expense item.

Comparing actual results to budgets gives a fuller picture of how things are going.

Assessing year-to-date performance only on actual figures ignores seasonal and other influences, and therefore is misleading.

For instance, take the first half of a financial year for a residential air conditioning supplier and installer.

The business anticipates paying half of their annual overheads, forty percent of employee costs, and making only fifteen percent of their yearly profit in that time.

If actual results match the budget, it gives confidence in continuing, despite the 'dismal' first-half figures.

Budgets are typically prepared for financial years and broken into months. They are matched against the regular accounting results to give a running year-to-date commentary.

Also useful are budget to actual reports for timeframes matching a project, market initiative, or season - any activity where monitoring progress helps show how things are going.

PREVIOUS YEAR COMPARISON

Lying the results for this month, and this year-to-date, alongside the same figures for last year, is interesting but not too informative.

Variations in the two years' figures are an undefined blend of expected and unexpected outcomes.

That is, rent is up, but that's because of the few extra car bays organised at the end of last year; power is up 15%, and that's a surprise because it usually rises about 5% per year.

A simple solution is to create a budget that starts with last year's actual results and then adjust to incorporate expected variations for the current year.

Comparing the month and year-to-date results to a budget shows immediately if things are going as anticipated - highlighting only unanticipated variations.

Merging expected and unexpected variations adds no useful knowledge while at the same time creating a fog obscuring valuable information.

CONTROLLING BUDGETS

Controlling budgets set expenditure limits, not expectations, and are used when authorisation gets delegated - principally by government and big business.

People responsible for administering those budgets have no power to set or vary them.

For instance, parliament provides government agencies with funds to undertake specified tasks to a specified standard each year. Each expense category has an amount that is the only money ever going to be available for it.

Not only can't the budgeted amount be exceeded, but the agency must spend all of it.

Occasionally controlling budgets have application for small businesses, such as delegating spending authority to a section, or project, manager.

The risk of this type of budget for regular business operations is the reinforcement it gives to spending money merely because it is within what has been allowed for, not because that expenditure makes sense.

Controlling budgets also block expenditure on unanticipated profitable opportunities. Such as not entering into a new sure-winner marketing campaign because there are no funds left in the advertising budget.

SALES BUDGETS

A sales budget is a trading strategy converted into dollars. It is a mix of product categories, targeted markets, and seasonal sales trends.

Overall sales budgets are more accurate if products get split into groups serving the same markets. It is easier to estimate expectations for each group individually, combining them at the finish to get the overall sales budget.

For instance, a car dealership could split the budget estimates between five categories; new car sales, used car sales, service centre, parts sales, and 'other'.

Each category will reflect its specific seasonal influences, marketing strategies, and historical patterns before combining all of them for a total sales budget.

Sales budgets provide a high-level view of future staff requirements, storage requirements, operational activity, and cash flow.

The ideal is to build a sales budget from the bottom up. That is by applying a budget to individual products, or tight groups of products, rather than total figures for broad categories.

The bottom-up approach allows mixing and matching figures to give detailed performance results for specific departments, markets, customer types, and outlets.

With enough detail to identify products according to profitability or sale strategies, it is possible to structure staff bonuses to reward sales only.

Budgets are tools for a huge range of operational insights. They give timely measures of whether things are going as planned.

Budgets benefit all businesses but are essential for new businesses, those undergoing significant change, and those with financial problems.

An operator uncertain of how their year is working out, without a budget, is like a sports fan watching their team's score but entirely ignoring the score of the other team.

22. PREMISES

OWN PREMISES
LEASES
OPERATING SUITABILITY
ONLINE BUSINESSES
CONSULTING & PROFESSIONAL BUSINESS
PASSING TRADE
SUB-LETS

A business with ideal premises has no difficulty operating in them, is visible and accessible to their market, has predictable and enforceable right to occupy, and can reach their optimum level of operations without moving.

'Ideal' is a remarkable scenario because so many operators choose their premises before beginning operations, or they buy an existing business with a lease in place (suiting someone else's plans).

The following sections illustrate commitments, operational limitations, and opportunities attaching to premises.

OWN PREMISES

This isn't about home offices or using the backyard shed; it's about using commercial premises owned by the operators or their families.

Using premises already owned solely by the operator avoids dealing with a landlord and utilises the asset.

If the operators buy the property specifically for the business, it is also an additional investment.

Using premises owned by family of the operators have benefits like flexibility on the term, are often cheaper, and have a landlord sympathetic to the personal circumstances of the operator.

Family tenancies are also problematic when they come without the clarity or security of a written lease, and sometimes even where they do. Few family disagreements get settled on commercial or legal grounds.

There are potential difficulties when not all operators own the property or are related to the owners. The unrelated become obliged to the related owners for concessions granted; also subject to personal and family influences over which they have no control.

LEASES

There are as many types and variations of leases as there are types and uses of properties, but as a general introduction, here are a few of the more common features:

The landlord arranges the preparation of the lease agreement, which is agreed to by the tenant, then registered with the courts. The tenant pays the stamp duty and legal preparation fees.

The agreement sets and binds obligations between the landlord and the tenant not otherwise covered by laws and regulations.

It is the full extent of agreed obligations between the parties; each can assume nothing.

Environmental, regulatory, and licensing obligations attaching to the property, or arising from operations, are not transferred from landlord to tenant or from tenant to landlord unless the agreement says so.

Standard agreements state the obligations landlord and tenant are each responsible for. They also say when the tenant reimburses the landlord for costs incurred, and vice versa.

The landlord recovers costs, such as local government rates, and repairs payable by the tenant, through a monthly charge for 'outgoings' on top of the standard monthly rent.

Shopping centres and malls have communal financial obligations and promotional costs, usually passed onto the tenant – often as part of the outgoings.

Lease agreements are frequently for three or five years, with further rights to renew for additional periods.

So, for example, the agreement may be a 5 + 5 + 5. Meaning, an initial lease of five years with an option to extend for a further five years, and that extended lease also has a five-year renewal option.

The renewed terms and conditions are the same as in the original agreement.

To keep lease rates in line with the market, but to avoid costs on valuations, rent increases usually take two forms within the one agreement:

- Either CPI or a fixed percentage increase as an interim step for a few years.
- A catch-up increase matching to a valuer's assessment of the lease value at review time, say, every third or fifth year.

For example, rent reviews in three-year rolling cycles of 4%, 4%, and market, then again 4%, 4%, market, etc., for the lease term and any extensions.

OPERATING SUITABILITY

Premises create rigid parameters to what is possible and how it will happen:

- The premises are where they are, and the floor area is what it is.
- Height clearance for the forklift can't be changed.
- Off-street parking needs to cater for staff and visitors.
- Semi-trailers require huge turning and loading space and create immovable blockages.
- Council and environmental restrictions are unchangeable.
- More inventory means larger storage spaces and delivery holding areas.
- Shelving doesn't go in front of windows.

Operational suitability for selling children's clothing in a shopping centre designed to retail light products involves little consideration. Maybe check for enough window display, an obscured storage and unpacking area, and acceptable compulsory trading hours imposed by the shopping centre management.

At the other end of the scale, operational suitability is a significant issue for a fabricator of steel structures, both for current operations and in being open to diversification.

Because leases are costly to get out of, and moving is disruptive, suitability needs assessing in both current terms and possible future directions.

ONLINE BUSINESSES

An online one-person consultancy or service does not need to commit to a location. So long as an internet connection is available, and working conditions are acceptable, the location is changeable.

Many online retailers have enough flexibility to operate from home, avoiding costs and commitment to a lease.

When extensive inventories, or equipment difficult to move, is involved, security of tenure is as important as it is for non-online businesses.

For instance, an online operator setting up equipment in the garage of the house they rent still needs a secure and predictable lease (on the house).

CONSULTING & PROFESSIONAL BUSINESS

To professions owing their patronage to location or reputation, exposure reminding the market of their existence is as important as it is to a retailer.

A surveyor located amongst a cluster of real-estate agents, property developers, and building engineers is seen by people right when needed.

A surveyor in a factory unit in a light industrial area needs huge exposure on other platforms or excellent industry contacts.

A urologist occupying rooms in a medical centre has medical professionals passing their door. This sub-conscious reminder, plus proximity, is valuable in generating new clients from these referral sources.

From a financial aspect, choosing a location for consulting and professional businesses comes down to a balanced blend of direct rent, media advertising costs, and personal promotion time.

LOCATION & PROMOTIONAL COSTS IN BALANCE

Premises with the best exposure and position cost more on rent but save on advertising and personal promotion costs.

PASSING TRADE

The number of people that pass by the premises is meaningless without further analysis:

- How many fit the demographic of the target market?
- How many are passing while it's open?
- Will seeing the premises influence their buying decision?
- If impulse buying is an issue, are they passing at a time that favours that impulse?
- How visible are the premises?
- What amount and form of signage is possible and permitted?

Being slaves to passing trade, service stations generally locate on high traffic routes with easy access, huge signs, and extensive lighting. But, regardless of the visibility and attractiveness, far fewer stop when the peak hour traffic is on the other side of the road.

Passing traffic must be within the market demographic and within the buyer's purchasing patterns.

Sub-lets

A sub-let is an arrangement to use premises leased by another business.

They range from casual verbal permission to use some spare space to a formal written agreement for a specific area; they might be for a specific time, task or ongoing operations.

Formal sub-tenancy agreements provide the same clarity of terms, rights, and obligations of any other lease. Still, not being a party to the lease with the landlord (the head lease) may not provide the same control over term extensions.

Casual sub-let arrangements offer a starting point for new businesses to prove their concept before committing to a formal long-term lease.

Also, strategic alliances form the basis of many sub-lets.

For instance, an appliance and air-conditioning installer sub-letting from an electrical retailer. Or a pathology service sub-letting space in a medical centre.

Sub-letting is a way to reduce costs for leaseholders with bigger premises than needed. It may be a long-term solution if they have the premises more for location than size. Or a short-term solution if they have spare space while they wait to expand into it.

For the primary leaseholder, sub-letting has the disadvantages of risking reputational damage by a failing of the sub-tenant; and the risks and inconvenience of having people on the premises not under their management.

Advantages and disadvantages of a space, location, presentation, neighbours, suburb, or accessibility are unique to every business.

It is virtually impossible to have everything exactly as wanted. Each aspect needs viewing as either 'essential' or 'desirable' when choosing premises.

The task is to achieve all essential elements, then blend and balance the desirable to the best overall advantage.

23. KEEPING THE BOOKS

WHAT TO RECORD

TAX OFFICE

EXTERNAL USERS

BOOKKEEPERS & ACCOUNTANTS

ACCOUNTING SOFTWARE

Bookkeeping has an annoying intolerance to errors and wild guesses; (almost) nobody likes doing it.

Businesses record things because they want to see how they're going, or an external authority requires it.

But 'the books' are not only listings of data and numbers to form part of a future picture, but also a use in themselves.

Bookkeeping includes unconnected listings for daily operations, names and contact details for suppliers and customers, records of employees' contact details, work rosters, and upcoming absences.

Bookkeeping is hugely valuable in providing a record of past daily sales, in any form, to help forecast the coming week's staffing and inventory requirements.

A log of actual events, timings, and tests carried out assists with resolving possible future disputes.

So, bookkeeping serves three distinct purposes:

- Management: daily operations and review of results to date,
- Compliance: an external authority requires them to, and
- Risk mitigation: to be able to prove what happened when disputes arise.

After determining the use, user, accuracy required, and when the data is needed, bookkeeping comes down to choosing the most appropriate way to collect, process, store, access, and report.

The following sections look at bookkeeping from a variety of perspectives.

WHAT TO RECORD

Accounting packages come pre-programmed with compliance elements as mandatory fields and management elements as optional fields.

For instance, a payroll system has mandatory fields to ensure:

- Recording of the employees' name, address, tax file number, gross wages, fringe benefits, tax withheld, and superannuation payments - required by the ATO.
- Actual hours worked are recorded - required by worker's compensation insurers.
- Details of the employee work classification, age, and relevant qualifications - required by agencies administering pay rates and employee conditions.

Optional fields will be available for recording the employee's telephone number, email address, and preferred name.

Knowing the elements required upfront enables combing all of them in one system, recording only what is relevant, and recording only once.

TAX OFFICE

The tax office dictates the records to be maintained and the supporting proof required for income tax and GST reporting.

And there are differences in the level of proof required between Income Tax laws and GST laws.

A supplier's invoice is not essential for income tax, but it is for making a GST refund claim.

The ATO also administers tax deducted from employees' wages, employees' compulsory superannuation contributions, and employees' fringe benefits. Each of these has specific recording and proof requirements.

The tax office has little tolerance for late lodgements and underpayments and puts the onus of knowing what is required squarely on the business.

Fines for non-compliance are deliberately punitive and system generated as a matter of course; there is no room for excuses or pleadings.

The tax office is the major driver of compliance bookkeeping. Operators either understand and comply or face demands for further detail and catch-up payments with severe penalties.

EXTERNAL USERS

Records needed are also driven by parties other than owners and authorities.

Lenders require timely reports on how operations are going, present asset values and how much is owing to others.

Lease or franchise agreements may include rights for the landlord and franchisor to receive specific financial information. Mostly this is turnover and buying details for calculating the rent, franchise fees or purchasing rebates.

Insurance claims for profits lost from an event that interrupted trading require detailed past operating figures for non-standard reporting periods and expense groupings.

When selling a business, the more confident a buyer is of the records' accuracy, the more likely they are to pay a premium price.

When the probability of needing unique information for a 'possible' user is remote and is obtainable retrospectively, it is enough to ensure the information remains easily identifiable within the regular records – to be retrieved if required.

BOOKKEEPERS & ACCOUNTANTS

Bookkeepers record what has happened, and accountants interpret those records and advise on financial strategies.

Such a clear distinction doesn't withstand one minute of reality amongst small businesses.

Both occupations develop knowledge on accounting systems, produce meaningful financial reporting, and know compliance issues for Income tax, GST, and payroll.

Accounting firms are obliged by their professional memberships to offer a comprehensive view of possibilities and financial strategies. Their professional status also makes them legally liable for losses a client incurs because of incorrect advice.

Bookkeepers, whether an employee or contractor, usually cost less than accountants.

Almost all accounting and bookkeeping firms register to lodge BAS with the tax office, giving more GST management options.

ACCOUNTING SOFTWARE

The accounting system becomes the core of computerisation in most small businesses.

The decision then is to what extent each accounting function integrates into the one package and to what extent other functions integrate with the accounting package.

For instance, both direct marketing campaigns and debt recording use customer information. Keeping separate records for each duplicates effort, causes inconsistencies, and access is clumsy and compartmentalised.

The alternative is integrated software modules for invoicing, marketing, banking, inventory, and accounting. With only one central source of data tables, details and history of every contact and transaction are available and updateable from mobile phones, tablets, and laptops.

Packages modified for specific business types exist. Full integration remains between basic modules with modifications or additional modules created to suit the industry.

Real estate agencies have packages integrating modules for rental management - linking property details, tenant records, the trust account, maintenance suppliers, standard forms, and workflows to monitor compliance with regulations.

Systems are available for repairers, manufacturers and fabricators that seamlessly flow information from job initiation to final billing. Others serve the unique record-keeping requirements of an industry.

General considerations in matching a system to a business are:

- Cost. The more integrated the system, and the more extensive its abilities, the more it costs.
- The skill required to maintain and update the system.
- The cost and availability of ongoing external system support.

- Existing familiarity with the system, both in-house and by external bookkeepers and accountants.
- System-specific training required, including cost and availability.
- The impact of temporary absences of a key operator.
- What are the advantages of moving from the existing system?
- How critical is constant internet access, and how reliable is service?
- Back-up plans: what restore data range options are included, and is there an off-site failsafe?
- In-built processing delays impacting customer service.
- Stability of the system developer and service provider regarding ongoing support and system updates?

Keeping the books is about having useful information when needed, accumulating valuable summaries of what has happened, complying with the demands of external agencies, and being able to prove it all.

The more comprehensively records are linked between functions, systems and operators, the less time it takes to operate, and a single source of truth for each data set means fewer mishaps.

The extent that records and functions are computerised and integrated across operations comes down to cost versus benefit.

It also comes down to the ability and willingness to dedicate the attention needed to support the IT systems.

24. BANKS

CHOOSING A BANK
COST OF BANKING
OPERATING ACCOUNT
LENDING FACILITIES

(This chapter looks at banks in general; the next two deal with making and receiving payments.)

'Bank' includes other financial institutions and online transaction management services when appropriate.

CHOOSING A BANK

Convenience is key.

Banks target market segments the same as any other business. From time to time, they focus their advertising on personal loans, housing loans, investment properties, businesses, or an offshoot product, offering an advantage over other banks on a specific product.

Over the long term and across the parcel of bank products, the cost and service levels will be similar across all banks, with the slightest convenience in operations outweighing total potential savings.

A business using cash has daily trips to the bank for deposits, perhaps by a deposit bag after hours, and for change for the tills; location, parking, and sense of security become primary issues.

So, branch premises become an influence and, therefore, the prospect of its permanency and trading days.

Past relationship with a bank offers the convenience of having identifications and possibly loan facilities in place – but that short-term advantage requires balancing with long-term operational benefits.

The personal image an operator has of a bank is not necessarily a business-related matter.

Any image the choice of bank projects to suppliers and customers is unpredictable, inconsistent, and hardly relevant as it occurs after any deal.

COST OF BANKING

Bank fees for having and operating the account are minor compared to other operating costs.

But visible bank charges are only part of the picture; each transaction also has implications for the amount and complexity of record-keeping and the time and complexity of daily operations.

The invisible flow-on costs of methods of paying and receiving money are significant and covered in the following sections. In a more general sense, invisible costs include:

- Processes around making online transactions.
- Downloading and accessing transaction and account details.
- Dealing with account administration issues and the flow of promotional paraphernalia from the bank.

- Multiple banks and multiple accounts, causing more daily data downloads, bank reconciliations and complex depositing and payment controls.
- Multiple banks causing extra travelling to deposit funds.

Dealing with one bank for all services reduces invisible costs enough to outweigh savings on individual direct charges gained by picking and choosing between providers.

OPERATING ACCOUNT

The central and pivot point of all financial dealings is a basic 'operating account'; fundamentally the same as everyday (non-savings) accounts operated by individuals.

The main difference between a business's and an individual's account is the number of people that need to operate or access it. For example, staff authorising payments, bookkeepers viewing and downloading transaction histories, and customers needing account details to make payments.

Using multiple operating accounts allows the separation of divisions and branches and, therefore, simple management of the banking functions of specific employees.

LENDING FACILITIES

There are loan arrangements designed specifically for businesses, but small business operators are likely also to use personal credit sources. The following overview covers both lending product categories.

Overdrafts are a floating line of credit attached to an operating account, usually used for working capital. The interest rate, calculated on the daily balance, fluctuates. The bank takes security for the maximum amount of the overdraft over business and personal assets.

A **term loan** is for a specific amount over a relatively long term. They have stated repayment amounts (usually monthly). Repayment amounts change occasionally because interest rates float.

Commercial loans generally fund the purchase of significant assets. Security may be on other assets entirely. Interest is pre-determined, with repayment in fixed monthly instalments of principal and interest combined.

Under **Hire purchase** agreements, assets are purchased by paying part of the cost upfront and borrowing the balance. The asset is the primary security. Interest is pre-determined, with principal and interest paid off in fixed monthly instalments.

The most regular use of **Finance leases** is to fund vehicles and other equipment. Essentially the lender buys the item and leases it to the business. No upfront payment is involved. Lease payments are a fixed monthly amount for a fixed term. The business pays out or refinances a specified percentage of the original purchase price at the end of the term.

Credit cards give instant unsecured credit. Usually, it is in the name of one of the owners and thereby moves the onus to repay to that person. Payments by cards with an interest-free payment period save overdraft interest for that (interest-free) period.

The repetition of banking functions, and the long-term nature of banking relationships, makes choosing bank services and their providers far more significant than dollars alone may indicate.

Deciding which services and providers to use requires balancing matters raised in this chapter with the following chapters on making and receiving payments.

25. MAKING PAYMENTS

CASH
BPAY
DIRECT CREDITS
DIRECTS DEBITS
CARDS
BUY NOW PAY LATER

How to make a payment!

CASH

Of all the standard payment methods, cash is by far the most inconvenient.

Having cash available to make a payment causes extra organisation around security and keeping enough on hand.

There is extra bookkeeping time and organisation around retaining the dockets and recording the payments.

Making payments from the till means extra effort balancing at the end of the day and recording them.

When payments for work-related expenses are from the personal cash of the operator, the risk of failing to record it soar. And, failing to record an expense means losing the GST refund and a tax claim, making it about forty-percent dearer.

Perhaps the only legitimate business-related reason for paying in cash is when there is such little trust from a supplier, they will only deal in cash.

BPAY

BPAY is an online payment service that is only an option when the supplier offers the service, and this is usually a relatively small portion of payments.

Payment is via the supplier's website or the business's bank or credit card accounts.

Algorithms behind the payment ID codes ensure exact identification of who is paying and what they are paying for. As a result, the risk of misidentification and delayed processing by the party receiving the payment is extremely low.

Payments via the supplier's website are usually the only available option when purchasing online; in other situations, it comes down to processing convenience and timing issues.

Paying via the supplier's website is convenient because it pre-fills the ID codes, but it also means going to each payee's website, and it doesn't offer the chance to schedule the payment for future dates.

BPAY payments made from the business's bank or credit card account mean careful transcriptions of ID codes. Still, it allows quicker processing when making multiple payments and gives the option to schedule the payment dates.

DIRECT CREDITS

Direct credit is a literal description of what the business making the payment does; they transfer funds from their bank to be credited directly into a supplier's bank account.

The payer, not the receiver, initiates the payment.

Funds leave the account immediately but take between an hour to the next day to arrive.

The New Payment Platform (NPP) and PayID have made significant improvements to direct credits.

The supplier is able to offer more straightforward identification than bank account details, making it more reliable to transcribe.

The transfer is instantaneous, allowing the seller to verify the receipt while carrying out the transaction.

The NPP also has 280 characters for payment description instead of the 18 characters of the old systems; therefore, improving chances of the receiver understanding who has made the payment and why they made it.

DIRECTS DEBITS

A direct debit is a payment that has come about from giving authority to a supplier to take (debit) payment directly from the business's bank account or credit card account.

The business receiving the payment (the supplier) initiates the transaction, not the customer making it.

It is a written agreement between both parties in a form approved by the supplier's bank. The supplier makes commitments to the bank to execute each direct debit transaction within strict guidelines.

Direct debits are used regularly for instalment type payments, such as loan repayments and insurance premiums.

Giving a supplier authority to take their monthly account payment directly can be a condition of trade – or be given in exchange for better trading terms.

Direct debits impose rigid payment schedules. It becomes more flexible if the debit is to a credit card account - the interim use of the credit card account gives a choice on when the funds leave the bank account.

CARDS

This is about using a card, in any manifestation, for on-the-spot purchases.

The ease of keeping a record of card payments is equal to BPAY, direct credits, and direct debits, but only if the account the card belongs to is accounted for in the books of the business.

Making a payment from a card not recorded in the books has the same risk of losing GST credits and paying extra tax. There is a record of the payment, but if the bookkeeper isn't aware of it, it's the same as not knowing about a cash payment.

BUY NOW PAY LATER

PayPal and Buy Now Pay Later (BNPL) payment arrangements are fundamentally retail oriented, with relatively low expenditure limits. As a result, they have limited application for business payments.

When used for a business item, the advantage of interest-free terms or extended payment time is not likely to outweigh the bookkeeping effort of remembering to record the purchase and doing so in instalments.

Extra thought in deciding which payment method to use makes recording more straightforward, more certain, and reduces the risk of confusion by the receiver.

26. RECEIVING PAYMENTS

CASH

EFTPOS

ELECTRONIC PAYMENT SERVICES

POST BILLPAY

HEALTH SERVICE PROVIDERS

DIRECT CREDITS

DIRECT DEBITS

There are so many ways to receive payments that few businesses offer all of them. So, which methods to offer?

Market norms will dictate the primary methods.

For example, a café that doesn't take cash and EFTPOS is restricting its market, and so too is an online retail site not accepting payment through its website.

Physical practicalities are a significant driver.

For example, in off-premise sites, when not enough security over staff and the money is possible. Or perhaps no internet is available, so electronic options are out.

Customer expectations of using a card that benefits them best mean the risk of loss of that customer if the card is not accepted.

And there is the need to weigh up the direct costs, recording time, complexity, staff training, security, and whether it needs to be available to all customers or across all parts of the business.

The following sections look at considerations in choosing which to offer.

CASH

Though it is usually unavoidable for retailers with a physical outlet, cash is a nuisance. For those with a choice, it is better to avoid, or at least minimise, it.

The cost of having a cash drawer, training staff, balancing the cash to the till, making bank deposits, and keeping the cash physically secure, make this a costly way to receive money.

It seems odd that some operators add a surcharge to low-value EFTPOS transactions but add nothing for cash transactions. The merchant fees, though visible, probably cost less than the direct and indirect costs of handling the cash.

Lesser skilled staff on the sales register is possible when there is no cash and only an EFTPOS terminal to operate.

There is less need to stand guard at the counter, and timing of the daily till count has more flexibility.

EFTPOS

EFTPOS is an acronym for Electronic Funds Transfer at Point of Sale.

It is a bit of software capable of analysing a code to channel a transaction to the financial service identified in that code.

Any terminal or device hosting that software processes all cards using that coding; it's just that the payments don't all go to the same bank or service provider.

Terminals are mainly rented from a bank, at a set monthly amount for each. The rent is separate from the bank's per-transaction fees (for the cards they represent), though it is on the same monthly bill.

Banks also provide less flexible terminals for a slightly higher fee per transaction but with no monthly rent.

EFTPOS is available from services that enable the use of a smartphone or tablet as a terminal. The fees per transaction are higher than the banks, but there is no terminal rent.

Using a personal device is cost-effective for occasional users (such as market stalls) and those receiving very few payments from non-business clients (such as tradies).

ELECTRONIC PAYMENT SERVICES

The most familiar of these are bank debit cards, Visa and Mastercard. However, there are many other cards, including BNPL and cards for interest-free plans.

For EFTPOS processing purposes, which card it is makes almost no difference, so long as it is a card the business accepts.

There are also service providers for remote electronic payments (non-EFTPOS) via the business's website, booking services, debt collecting services, or selling agent sites.

For electronic payment types a business is obliged to offer, the costs attaching are an inescapable part of operations. For optional methods, the following points merit consideration:

- What the customer will do if the payment type is not available.
- How much extra bookkeeping is involved in having another payment service provider depositing into the bank account.
- Charges by the service provider, both per transaction and any other.

- How long before the money appears in the bank account.
- Is each payment received deposited individually in the bank account or bundled into one deposit for the day or period?
- Are per-transaction fees deducted from the amount deposited?
- How easy is it to get details of the individual customer payments for each bank deposit and the actual fee deducted for each payment?
- For booking and other payment and collection services, how available is information on payments as they're made - without waiting to see the deposit in the bank account?

There are accounting packages linking to specific online receipting services that automatically integrate those receipts into the accounting package. These are not broadly applicable.

POST BILLPAY

Post Billpay is a money collection service from Australia Post. It offers a street-front presence throughout Australia for customers to pay in cash or by card.

Collecting payments through post offices gives access to retail customers reluctant or unable to make payments online.

It is also an alternative to collecting payments at all at the premises, saving time and the need to have trained staff and receiving facilities in place.

Post Billpay also offers online payment options.

Payments collected by Billpay, either through a post office or online, are accumulated into one daily total and deposited directly to the bank account.

Billpay deducts their charges and then send the net amount to the business.

HEALTH SERVICE PROVIDERS

Businesses, or practitioners, that raise fees to patients subject to reimbursement from Medicare can process their claim electronically and have the money credited directly to their bank account.

Services are also available to lodge claims for the patient's private health fund's contribution electronically with the health fund and receive immediate payment.

Many electronic health service reimbursements don't transact through standard EFTPOS terminals.

These are specialist services that, although not necessarily straightforward, are generally understood by operators through their existing familiarity with their field.

DIRECT CREDITS

This service is a standard function of banks and therefore takes no action to have it available; businesses need only provide their bank account details or PayID to the customer.

Customers make an online instruction to their bank to transfer money from their account to the business's bank account.

Each direct credit appears as a separate transaction on the bank statement with a description added by the customer.

Direct credits from the traditional method take between an hour and overnight to arrive. There are 18 characters of description for the sender to use.

Direct credits via the New Payment Platform (NPP) arrive instantly, and the description field is two hundred and eighty characters.

On the plus side, there are no direct charges for direct credits and no establishment effort.

On the negative side, the business is at the mercy of the customer's description to identify the purpose of the direct credit.

Because of the lack of control over the deposit's description, processing in the books can't be fully automated.

DIRECT DEBITS

Banks provide direct debit facilities enabling a business to take payment from their customer's bank account directly.

Many people pay loans, insurances, and annual membership fees in this manner.

The business's bank provides this facility and enforces the safeguards to the account debited.

There is an initial effort around signing up for the service and customising the customer's agreement forms, and there are ongoing fixed and variable fees.

For each direct debit, the business effectively guarantees they have a properly executed agreement with the customer.

The bank accepts instructions to debit a list of bank and credit card accounts, with the amounts stated, and immediately deposits (credits) the list's total into the business's account.

The bank automatically reverses the amount of any direct debit that fails.

Because the business has generated the transaction description, not the customer, it has enough reliability to process by automation.

Direct debits encourage more sales by enabling payment by instalments and is also helpful in enforcing payment plans for defaulted debtors.

Also, control over a customer's payment encourages more favourable trading.

The choice of which methods of receiving payments to use comes down to three questions:

Is it usable: driven by security, availability, and operator inclination and capabilities?

Is it needed: what are customer expectations, and how does it fit in with other methods offered?

Which provider: which service provider has the most beneficial way of delivering and reporting the receipts?

27. INSURANCE

COMPULSORY COVER
WORKERS COMPENSATION
PUBLIC LIABILITY
ASSETS
LOSS OF PROFITS
INCOME PROTECTION
PROFESSIONAL INDEMNITY

Insurance is an element of continuance planning - protection against losing the business when something disastrous happens.

It is about getting funds for a replacement or emergency funds in times of dire need.

It is, therefore, as much about protecting the whole business as it is about covering single risks.

Because of the whole-of-business aspect, operators generally deal with a single broker or agent and have detailed annual reviews.

COMPULSORY COVER

Taking cover is not always a free choice.

Cover may be compulsory because of regulations, such as workers compensation and compulsory third-party vehicle insurance.

It may be a condition of holding a professional membership, such as professional indemnity insurance.

Or, it might be in the terms of an agreement, such as a lease stipulating window and public liability cover.

When it is declared compulsory, the next elements in the decision are:

- Is there is a choice on which insurer to use?
- What risks must it specifically cover?
- What is the minimum cover required?

WORKERS COMPENSATION

Each state and territory make workers compensation insurance for all employees compulsory covering income and care costs if they suffer a work-related injury or illness.

The governments either administer the insurance themselves or dictate the provider and the extent of cover.

Whether or not a person is an employee needs careful consideration. The definition of an employee for workers compensation is not the same as it is for income tax or industrial law purposes.

For instance, a subcontractor on a daily rate and working under direction, and as a GST subcontractor for income tax purposes, is classified as an employee for workers compensation purposes.

Cost varies according to the risks associated with each employee's occupation – the higher the risk of a claim, the higher the premium.

A business's history of claims also influences the cost of the premium.

Premiums are calculated on estimated annual wages, for each work category, for a year in advance. When actual figures are available at the end of the year, the premiums get calculated accurately, resulting in a refund or make-up payment.

Usually, financing plans are available to spread the premium payment over the year.

PUBLIC LIABILITY

A business has a legal responsibility not to do, or fail to do, anything that causes harm to a person or property; this is their public liability.

There doesn't need to have been deliberate action or neglect.

The consequences of a public liability failing can be catastrophic, with claims extending to millions of dollars.

Landlords, lenders, major suppliers, and others with a significant stake in the continuance of a business may make a stated amount of public liability cover a condition of any arrangement. A minimum cover of ten-million dollars or more is not uncommon.

Fortunately, it is relatively cheap insurance, and insurers will generally bring attention to it or offer it wrapped up with other cover.

ASSETS

Just as families insure their house, contents, cars, jet-ski, and caravan, businesses insure their 'tangible' assets.

The approach is similar, but the speediness of getting a replacement in place has much different considerations.

Asset insurance generally provides either cash compensation for the value lost or the cost of an equivalent replacement. It does not (unless stated) cover any loss of profits caused by the event.

Cover is available for the risk of loss or damage to customers' property the business is working on or has possession of.

When operating on other premises and sites, cover is available for the business's tools, equipment, and materials incorporated into the customer's property but still legally owned) by the business.

Without a plan for the immediate use of a replacement for critical equipment, taking out insurance on that equipment may leave the operator with cash but no ability to operate.

LOSS OF PROFITS

Loss of profits insurance ensures ongoing income when unable to operate, or only partially operate, due to any of a pre-agreed list of events happening.

Stopping or slowing operations reduces turnover, but it also reduces the cost of goods sold and overheads; so, the claim is for loss of net profit – not turnover.

The events also create costs of their own.

Therefore, a loss of profits claim is the sum of:
- Net profit lost - estimated from past financial reports.
- Unavoidable ongoing charges - payments that remain necessary whether fully operating or not.

  They include rent, essential wages, interest, power, and registrations.
- Additional costs incurred - depending on the event and cover arranged.

  For instance, temporary fencing and security patrols while the premises are damaged, costs of notifying customers, off-site storage, and penalties for failure to meet contractual targets.

Choosing to take this cover comes down to weighing its cost and the potential claim amount against the cost of closure or alternate trading possibilities.

Businesses without loss of profits insurance are simply accepting the risk of funding losses from their own resources.

Loss of profits insurance does not cover lost profits resulting from sicknesses and personal injuries of the operators.

INCOME PROTECTION

Income protection insurance is a form of limited workers compensation cover for the self-employed.

It is common amongst tradies, personal service providers, consultants, and operators with no income if they can't work because of sickness or accident.

But, usually, it's about protecting the lost income, not covering medical and other costs to restore the person to working capacity. In this respect, it is significantly different to workers compensation.

Premiums vary according to:

- The sicknesses and events covered.
- The amount of cover required.
- The lag period before compensation commences (for example, 28 days).
- The number of months cover continues.
- Lump-sum options for permanent disabilities.

Accident-only cover is available, which suits the cash-strapped with confidence in their health and fitness. It also suits operators with health issues that make sickness cover unattainable or too expensive.

PROFESSIONAL INDEMNITY

Suppliers of professional skills, knowledge, or advice can be held legally responsible for losses arising from incorrect, inappropriate, or inadequate advice. Insurance against this risk is called Professional Indemnity (PI).

Businesses requiring PI include medicos of all persuasions, solicitors, architects, accountants, building surveyors, travel agents, real estate agents, and valuers.

PI covers the costs of defending negligence claims and any damages and penalties in the event of losing or settling those claims.

A stated minimum level of PI is often compulsory for services provided under the banner of a professional body and for government-regulated occupations.

For occupations with expensive PI, the cost of minimum compulsory cover makes starting up a costly risk, and, operating part-time uneconomic.

Repeated claims by a policyholder, or significant claims across an occupation, can make premiums rise massively from one year to the next.

And, insurers occasionally refuse cover to individual policyholders or an entire profession.

Compulsory PI brings a significant element of uncertainty.

Insurance either enables continuance after a damaging event or, at least, protects the owners' finances.

Although subject to normal cost versus benefits judgement, the premium's cost is already proportionate to the industry's history of risk and consequences.

If it's a truly low risk, with survivable consequences, it reflects in a low premium cost. If it's a high cost, it usually means it's essential.

28. OTHER MATTERS

TAX OFFICE REGISTRATIONS
REGISTRATIONS AND AFFILIATIONS
SKILLS DEVELOPMENT
CONSISTENT IMAGE
SECURITY
CLEANING AND GARDENING

The following are a collection of items that haven't warranted a chapter of their own yet are still worth attention.

TAX OFFICE REGISTRATIONS

Point # 1: No business can operate without an Australian Business Number (ABN). ABNs come from being listed in the Australian Business Register (ABR), which the tax office manages.

Point # 2: No business can employ anyone without registering as an employer with the tax office.

(Points 1 & 2 combined give the tax office almost watertight traceable links between all business-to-business and business-to-employee payments.)

GST is another registration, separate from entry on the ABR, although both registrations are possible on the one application.

To be clear:

- Entry on the ABR is compulsory.
- GST registration is compulsory for businesses with an annual turnover of more than a specified minimum (threshold) amount[11].
- GST Registration is optional under that specified minimum (threshold) amount.
- The tax office administers both ABR and GST registrations together, but they are separate issues.

Even though they're under the compulsory threshold, businesses in the establishment stage sometimes register for GST to get GST refunds on their start-up equipment purchases.

REGISTRATIONS AND AFFILIATIONS

There are required permits, registrations, and affiliations associated with almost all businesses.

They can cover work undertaken, goods carried, materials used, localities accessed, images used, music played, chemical discharges, etc.

Some are so obscure or industry-specific that only consultations with industry advisors or other operators expose them.

But, to build an operation without the required permits and registrations is to risk sudden closure, massive interruption to operations, and financial penalties.

Affiliations with professional, industry, or local commerce bodies gives access to advice from people that understand the owner's viewpoint.

---

[11] The threshold for compulsory GST registration is subject to changes - the current level is readily available from the ATO's website.

Affiliations also provide networking opportunities that benefit operators in terms of personal knowledge and developing trade opportunities.

Affiliation with respected professional and industry bodies increases credibility in the eyes of prospective customers.

SKILLS DEVELOPMENT

Time and money spent on improving skills is not so much a cost as it is a loss to profit and future security if not undertaken.

Products change, systems evolve, customer expectations change, the market environment changes, and efficiencies emerge; nothing remains constant.

Suppliers are a valuable source of product knowledge, and customers are a source of movement in product demands. Still, both these sources have their limits; broader market trends and product directions come from accessing knowledge external to those sources.

In professions and skills-based advisory services, the need for constant knowledge and skills improvement is obvious and unavoidable.

It is easy to postpone setting aside the time and direct expenses of skills development, or fail to do enough, indefinitely. But the cost is a change to the image in the market from 'state-of-the-art' to 'out-of-date'.

When an image slips, future growth needs to come from generic growth in its existing customer base because less will come from market referrals and reputation.

CONSISTENT IMAGE

Customers use their image of the business to form expectations of how dealings will be.

No matter how subconsciously the customer sees situations or actions contradicting this expectation, each challenges their view.

Even over-delivering contradicts their expectations, though probably for a positive outcome.

Keeping customers focused on the image wanted means ensuring no situation or action they meet contradicts that image.

Inconsistencies can be accidental, such as a signwriters' ute with a spelling error in its signage. Or, more underlying such as signage promoting a state-of-the-art image, written in a style in vogue ten years ago.

A boutique clothing boutique that promotes a trendy image would completely get rid of all last season's stock – and the in-store music would be of a style and volume liked by people likely to buy the clothing.

A shop selling mobility aids for seniors would have convenient parking bays, no stairs into the shop, no loud rap music playing, well-trained staff, evidence of support for causes relevant to seniors, and a product delivery and assembly service.

Maintaining an image takes monitoring; for instance, a service provider promoting itself as being fast and reliable would have performance indicators to monitor how fast and reliable it is.

Businesses promoting an image of low prices monitor the prices of competitors.

Periodic customer surveys monitor whether the targeted image appropriately links the market and the business's strategies.

Negative effects from contradicting an image can be greater than the advantages of that image.

For instance, a real estate firm promoting clean and green with its name emblazoned across a giant V8 SUV loses more from the offensive contradiction than the (barely business-related) promotion gains them.

SECURITY

No business is so simple that security is irrelevant.

Even an online part-time business selling handmade goods needs security over the business name, updates to the site, customer name and payment details, and intellectual property attaching to the goods.

When it comes to security over physical property, it needs to be relevant to what is most important:

- If stopping it from happening is a priority, window grills, quality locks, clear and well-lit surrounds, and sensors and cameras monitored in real-time would be relevant.
- Unmonitored video surveillance and stock counts are relevant when discovery, retribution, and punishment are priorities.
- When financial compensation is a priority, insurance is the answer.

The need for security against dishonesty can't be assessed from the operators' knowledge of what is, and is not, valuable; it's the wrongdoer's view that counts.

On a risk versus return basis, an owner might consider it irrational to break in to steal the $200 till float. But not everyone is rational all the time, and not everyone knows how little cash is in the till.

So, the front door gets smashed, till wrecked, money taken, and the thieves, being so frustrated at such a lousy haul, steal stock and vandalise the premises on their way out.

Security is also about guarding against accidental loss. For instance, keeping a backup of the data, systems, and operational guides off-site protects those things from damage to the premises.

Security is also allocating unique user IDs to staff members as a deterrent to improper use of the systems or tracing the creator of inaccurate or dishonest transactions.

CLEANING AND GARDENING

When cleaning and gardening are about presentation to customers, it is because a cost versus benefit analysis has shown it to be worthwhile.

In doing that analysis, a particular vision is in the operator's mind, and that vision is the targeted standard.

Whether through enthusiasm, concerns about the costs, or indifference, the existing cost versus benefit result is made irrelevant by departing from that standard.

A café setting up a garden would picture its appeal based on an image of mature plants. To save upfront costs by buying immature plants is to delay that appeal for the two or three years it takes to achieve that picture.

The loss of extra trade during the period without the targeted standard will probably be greater than the savings on the plants.

When that café also decides a clean glass front door and windows would increase trade and starts cleaning them once a week, it also acknowledges that having a dirty door and windows for the other five or six days is damaging business.

Whatever the activity, it must be within the objectives of the business.

If it doesn't produce a net benefit, it is either a failed business decision or a personal objective that needs re-thinking.

29. BUSINESS GROWTH

COST OF GROWTH
WAYS TO GROW
WHEN TO GROW
ALTERNATIVES

Growth means getting bigger, buying larger capacity production equipment, opening another outlet, taking on more fee-earning staff, or branching out into other products.

It might be from deliberate planning, unavoidable, wanted or not, the best thing to happen, or a poor choice on where to direct time and money.

But growth is only good when it improves the owners' lives and is within their financial capacity.

The worst kind of growth is the unconscious type, where goals aren't re-assessed after reaching their business plan targets. Or get led blindly into actions from external influences, such as suppliers aiming to increase their own sales.

Passing up, or not recognising, desirable growth opportunities is as poor a choice as unnecessary growth. And, not growing when competitors are, risks declining sales as the competitors take a larger market share.

Here are aspects of growth.

COST OF GROWTH

Adding a range of products and services, or increasing the number, size, or type of outlets, is akin to starting again from scratch.

Existing operations continue course while the 'new business' operates alongside on a different life cycle, with entirely different cash flow patterns and management demands.

Not all costs of a new range of products or services are separately identifiable, such as:

- Inventory carrying costs.
- Supplier contact time.
- Storage and display space.
- Manufacturing moulds, dies, patterns, re-tooling, etc.
- Extra staff and staff training.
- Special packaging.
- New handling equipment.
- Advertising and promotion.
- Updating and expansion of online platforms and outlets, and physical signage.
- Bookkeeping and IT system adaptations.
- Registrations, permits and licences.
- Risk exposure and insurances.

Under-funding the growth and running out of money, thereby damaging existing operations, is another cost.

Cash flows for growth projects are usually separate from existing cash flow forecasts, and owners risk not recognising critical shortages coming from when both predictions have low points at the same time.

Despite the growth project having its own character, the business has only one cash flow - combining the two cashflows gives a more realistic view.

Significant commitments are often attached to new products or services, which become costly if the venture fizzles rather than prospers.

The commitments might be a requirement to carry a minimum range and quantity, a minimum display space, a stated advertising and promotion budget, prohibition from carrying competing products, personal guarantees, or higher costs per unit when not meeting targets.

There is also an opportunity cost of committing 'spare' management capacity to a marginally worthwhile venture. In other words, proceeding with plan A while plan B (a month away from presenting itself) is a much better proposition.

WAYS TO GROW

Four basic growth categories are organic, more investment, vertical expansion, and horizontal expansion.

Organic growth is making operations larger by doing the same thing, only more of it. It is usually gradual and driven by building on existing strengths and existing markets. It is funded chiefly from profits and, to this extent, if not constrained, causes ongoing cash flow problems despite being profitable.

Further investment injected. Such as funding for campaigns to develop new markets, bigger and better production equipment, technology upgrades, better premises, or upskilling the workforce.

Vertical expansion is taking on a function that feeds into or out of the business. For a vehicle panel beater, it is gearing up also to do motor trimming. For an online retailer of flat-pack furniture, it is setting up a bricks and mortar outlet to sell assembled furniture.

Horizontal expansion is doing more of what is already happening. It includes increasing existing capacities and increasing the size of operations to take advantage of the economies of scale. For instance, one of two pharmacies in a regional town buying out and closing the other - achieves twice the gross profit with (relatively) minor increases in salaries and overheads.

WHEN TO GROW

The first thing to establish is, why grow?

Is it to make more money, maintain market position, reach a more efficient operating level, or perhaps from a sense of competitiveness?

Is it driven by long-term objectives such as the business's eventual sale or room for more family employment?

Before committing resources, operators must consider whether their products and services, and the markets they are selling into, are developing or declining.

Growth in a declining market risks having a declining income to service the debt and a larger capital loss eventually.

A declining market still has opportunities. The business may get a larger share of the smaller market as competitors retreat, also making higher margins possible.

While a developing market has obvious growth opportunities, it also risks larger players getting into it and taking the growth and more.

ALTERNATIVES

Profit comes from a mix of volume, margins, and overheads.

Focusing on volume, as is common, risks overlooking margins and overheads, both of which are also powerful contributors to growing profits.

Achieving higher margins from an image makeover increases profits without changing the volume sold, and without increasing (other) overheads.

Increased profits are possible from reviewing overheads and finding efficiencies such as using IT in place of manual processes, downsizing premises, sub-letting spare space, and reducing staff.

Within an owners' overall mix of assets and investments, channelling more resources to the business requires balancing with other parts of their lives' needs and opportunities.

And, diversifying to investments outside of the business spreads risk and future growth opportunities over a broader front.

Growth needs approaching with care because the costs are never entirely visible and come in many forms, adding pressures not readily identified as having been driven by that growth.

Growth to increase profits or ensure continuance is usually desirable and even necessary, but not always.

Unconscious and unplanned growth is the enemy of a solid business and a balanced lifestyle.

30. THE BIG PICTURE

PERSONAL VALUES
STANDARD PRINCIPLES
UNDERSTANDING THE MARKET
MISLEADING TRUISM

Every business decision changes the mix of the concoction that will become the future.

So, despite having solid logic, if a choice doesn't work in harmony with the general flow of decisions, the future develops in unexpected ways.

Clear overarching principles are the answer. Here are a few to think about.

PERSONAL VALUES

Businesses are about producing money, both present income and accumulating wealth. Arguments against this statement are personal ones!

But each decision has a personal value, measurable by how much it supports or conflicts with personal interests.

Operators without clear thought on when leisure, the personally satisfying aspects of the business, or any spare mental bandwidth, are more important than an extra dollar, are constantly conflicted.

They are also in danger of creating a monster.

Having enough dollars is non-negotiable, but from then on, it's all choice!

STANDARD PRINCIPLES

Standard operating processes and principles are essential; there are better things to do than constantly re-evaluate alternatives for repetitive choices and actions.

But markets change, product and service choices evolve, new tools and processes become available, and even the personal values of the operator get updated.

Standard operating processes and principles eventually choke operations.

Find any negative, find the cause or action behind it, and decide if a habit or driving thought needs altering.

Put in place a discipline for occasional or cyclical reviews of tasks executed using standard processes and principles.

Also, be alert for external indicators and benchmarks to reveal faulty habits and thoughts. Clues may be as vague as a conversational aside by a customer, supplier, employee, or family member.

UNDERSTANDING THE MARKET

When an operator speculates, or knows intuitively, what the market wants and how it will react, they have just completed a market survey of one.

Certainly not a survey size deserving of investment.

Surveying customers gives a better view of their needs and wishes. But this is only a partial survey of the market – not a reliable picture of the whole market.

Rather than survey customers alone, there is value in understanding why the other part of the market are not customers.

Whenever forming an opinion on a market, without clear evidence of the facts, be acutely aware of how inadequate the survey size is.

MISLEADING TRUISM

Perseverance, resilience, and willpower are essential to success; an inspiring mantra, especially when the going gets tough.

Unfortunately, perseverance, resilience, and willpower are equally as likely to be present in failure, maybe not essential to it, but present.

The real issue is to what those three elements get applied. Trying hard isn't the same as doing the best thing.

Perseverance, resilience, and willpower create the most insidious type of losses; the passing up of better opportunities, bigger profits, or the chance to work less for the same money.

When more perseverance, resilience, or willpower is needed, it's time to check if the business is heading in the best direction.

The past and present are interesting – maybe predictive, but never instructive!

31. CONCLUSION

THE TAKE-AWAY

PARTING THOUGHT

How's this for a summary:

- Going into business has many facets but is not complicated.
- There is much decision making between choices that first need discovering.
- No situation has only one dimension.
- No decision is good for all times or all situations.

It's true; there is endless navigating through rules and influences outside of an operator's control, yet all subjects worked through became basic after shining light on them.

Business is not a thing in its own right; it's simply a way of making income, living life, and preparing for the future; operators are free to bend and shape it any way they wish.

More productive and less stressful though, when that bending and shaping results from conscious and balanced thinking!

THE TAKE-AWAY

If reading this book was motivated by thoughts of starting a business, and that's still the plan, set out the bones of a plan –

and flesh it out with priorities and costs clearly in mind. Tackle the deal breakers first.

If reading has been as a refresher of current business approaches, surely it has jolted enough thoughts to initiate improvements. Or perhaps it will encourage mentoring of others.

For other readers, hopefully, it has given an overview of the principles and the day-to-day workings behind why businesses do what they do.

Under the sheer number of approaches this book has shown to everyday issues, there is another, underlying, message:

Whatever your view, no matter how logical and supportable, it will not be the only logical and supportable view. Look for the others – choose the one that serves best.

PARTING THOUGHT

Essentially an employee puts in the effort and attitude they think appropriate and waits to see what fate (their boss or industry) deals up to them: little risk and limited responsibility for outcomes.

Business operators have ultimate responsibility, even for things outside of their control. If they can't change the situation, they change the way they deal with it.

They have incredible highs and crushing lows; toil happily in a satisfying work-lifestyle balance or find themselves trapped in unrewarding work.

But, that element of responsibility, having such input and control over destiny, is the biggest positive of owning a business.

Have a great one!

32. CHAPTERS & SECTIONS